JIMMY & LAURA SEIBERT

PARENTING

WITH OUT

REGRET

RAISING KIDS WITH PURPOSE, NOT PERFECTION

PARENTING WITHOUT REGRET

Published by Clear Day Publishing, a division of Clear Day Media Group LLC, Waco, TX. cleardaypublishing.com.

Published in association with Lux Creative {theluxcreative.com}

ISBN: 978-0-9863734-2-8

Library of Congress Control Number: 2015951813
Cover Design: Kyle Rogers
Interior Design: Lux Creative {theluxcreative.com}
Printed in the United States of America.

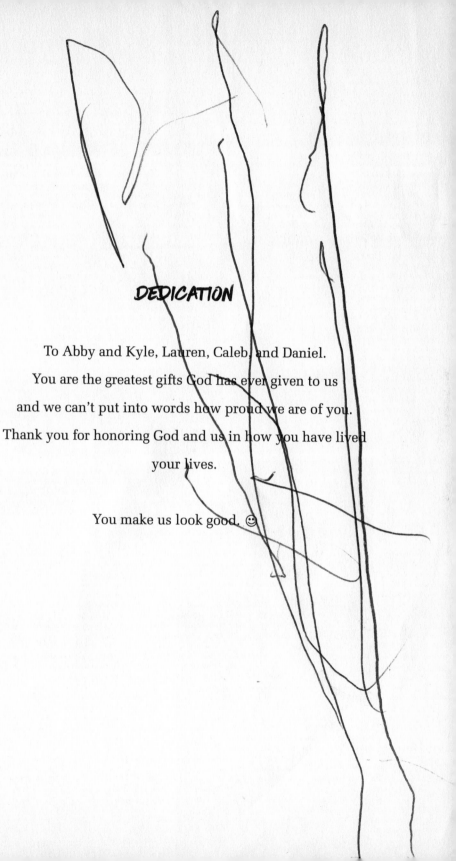

DEDICATION

To Abby and Kyle, Lauren, Caleb, and Daniel.

You are the greatest gifts God has ever given to us

and we can't put into words how proud we are of you.

Thank you for honoring God and us in how you have lived

your lives.

You make us look good. ☺

TABLE OF CONTENTS

PREFACE

We started this project with great reluctance: How can we teach about parenting when our kids are still in process? How can we talk about how to do parenting when we are still in the journey ourselves? These are the big questions and vulnerabilities we have felt in writing this book.

But as always, our friends and church community have continued to encourage us to not only love and honor God with our personal lives, but to help anyone we can with whatever we've learned. One thing we've learned is that raising these kids required not only our commitment, but also the investment of others in our kids' lives, from Sunday School teachers to youth workers to friends and extended family.

We have tried to communicate in this book what we felt were the most important keys in raising kids who will end up loving God, loving each other, and be on mission in our world. A lot of our input came from our kids themselves. They not only affirmed our main points but also gave great insight and practical input about what they feel has worked well.

On a very practical note, this project would never have been possible without a few people who have to be mentioned here:

> Our long-term personal assistant and dear friend, Mary Greenwald, has spent hours sitting side by side with us going through different drafts, answering questions, and encouraging us when we were down. Her love and faithfulness, prayers and support have not only made this project possible, but have allowed us to be who God has called us to be in every area of life and ministry.

Drew Steadman, our Director of Ministry, has not only been our advocate but has spent hours and hours going through drafts of manuscripts, helping us to get clear on our message and to communicate it in the best way possible.

Another one of our coworkers, Robert Fuller, helped us make sure it was not boring. His practical and creative input made this book better and more readable.

Rachel Lee and Kim Bullajian were instrumental in getting us started on this project by working on our outline and giving us vision for what this book could be. Thank you for your love and patience.

Jeff Abshire, our long-term right-hand man, spent time editing the manuscript and supporting us personally to get this project done for the betterment of our church community.

And last but not least, this project would not have come to fruition without the wonderful and sacrificial leaders and investors at Clear Day Publishing. Thank you for believing in us and this project.

The list could go on and on of people who have read the manuscript, given us feedback and insight, and helped us to be better parents. But ultimately, we know that it has been the grace of God, and the power of the Holy Spirit that has given us both the strength and the wisdom that we needed to raise our kids.

INTRODUCTION

I stood in the foyer of First Baptist Church with our oldest daughter on my arm as we waited to walk through the sanctuary doors. Over one thousand people were gathered to celebrate her marriage. The moment was deeply emotional as I reflected on the past twenty-two years of parenting. I remembered holding Abby as a newborn and, years later, running alongside her while she learned to ride a bike. I recalled our little dates walking down the street holding hands, and I thought back to countless conversations we shared as we navigated junior high and high school. I was about to put her life into the hands of the man that Laura and I had prayed for all her life, a man we trusted and believed could take her further on this great adventure with God. This sacred moment was a milestone, the fulfillment of a part of our calling as parents. It was emotional, and yet deeply satisfying. It was rewarding for Laura and me to reach this moment with joy and expectation, and with very few regrets.

Twenty-two years earlier we had made the decision that if God would give us children, we would give our lives to raising those children to love Him and to honor Him. We were not simply adding raising kids to the checklist of our lives; it would become one of the central parts of our calling.

This commitment didn't come cheap. We wrestled with the question of how to embrace our vocational calling with our calling as parents. We soon realized that our commitment would require a sacrifice on our behalf. We consistently evaluated our lives to make sure that our kids were a top priority. We had to sacrifice our time and rearrange our schedules if needed. We sacrificed our finances by choosing to invest in their education, family vacations, and mission trips instead of just investing in worldly possessions.

We don't regret missing career opportunities, owning fewer possessions, or giving up our own personal free time. The richness of our relationships with our kids far exceeds any of that. In the moment, while changing diapers or dealing with discipline, it was hard to maintain perspective. There were times we felt so overwhelmed that we wondered if we would make it as parents. But perspective comes with time—and boy does it go fast! Here we sit, two decades later, not only having few regrets for the sacrifices we made, but actually wishing we had invested even more. As I stood there giving away our daughter in marriage, I knew that every sacrifice we had made was worth it.

Weddings and funerals are powerful life events that call us back to perspective. Weddings mark the beginning of a new family and build upon the foundations that were laid, or the lack thereof. Funerals highlight the fullness of a life lived. What I know, after years of pastoring, is that what people care about in those moments are sons and daughters, brothers and sisters, mothers and fathers, and close friends who have hung together through thick and thin, who have loved deeply, sacrificed abundantly, and served the mission of God fully.

Many people have asked Laura and me to share the story of how we have raised our kids. So this is OUR story. Every person, couple, and family will have their own unique journey. We are sharing ours with you, not as a prescription for every situation that arises, or a perfect formula for how to parent, but as a story to fill you with hope.

Don't get us wrong. This is not about perfection or the inability to fail. We all have regrets and make mistakes. But it's about living and parenting with intentionality so you won't regret the focus and effort that you put into raising your kids. Ultimately our prayer is that as we look back in our latter days, we are not consumed by thoughts that we wished we had done things differently, but rather are thankful that we had parented wholeheartedly.

CHAPTER 1

PARENTING FROM WHOLENESS

If we confess our sins, He is faithful and righteous to forgive us our sins and to cleanse us from all unrighteousness.
1 John 1:9

LAURA

The summer after my freshman year of college, everything fell apart. On the outside I seemed to have it all together. I finished my first year with excellent grades. I pledged a sorority and made many new friends. No one would have guessed on the inside I was in turmoil, my insecurity so intense I began to starve myself.

A consistent lie loomed in my heart: *You will never be enough.*

As these words attacked me over and over again, insecurity and self-consuming thoughts about who I was, and who I wasn't, eventually led to an all-out struggle with anorexia.

Looking back on my childhood, it's easy to say I grew up in a stable home. We had no real traumas or major outward dysfunction. My father and mother stayed faithful to each other for the duration of their marriage and did their best to raise me and my two brothers well. As far as I can remember, we never had a material need that was not met. My father was very responsible, generous, and hardworking. He was the first in his family to go to college and made it his aim to be an excellent provider in every way for his family. These qualities still influence my life today, and I honor him for that. However, he had a demanding job that caused him to work long hours, and he was not around a lot. And because he was not much of a talker, at least not on a heart level, he wasn't very present in my emotional development. Because a father is a key factor in how a little girl shapes her identity (especially an emotional girl like me), I grew up with a question mark on my heart as to whether I was valued, wanted, or pretty. If my father had really known my emotional needs, I believe he would have done his best to meet them. But because of time, the demands of his job, and his own lack of awareness, this wasn't the case. By my late teenage years I found myself confused and struggling.

Many of you might have had the same kind of experience. There are wounds from your past that you can't seem to recover from. The good news is that God is the Healer. He can heal every wound, no matter how deep and debilitating, and no matter if they were put there willfully, or as in my case, in innocence. Thankfully, God intervened.

In the middle of my sophomore year of college I had a significant encounter with God. A good friend and I were

8

spending the evening praying, and one by one, the Holy Spirit showed me the lies that had been plaguing me for years. In that prayer time, He replaced those lies with His truth. I began to renew my mind with who God says I am and not who I felt I was. The dark cloud that covered my mind and enslaved my thoughts started to dissipate. Over a period of time, I experienced increasing levels of healing, and in turn, freedom from the anorexia.

During this time, God introduced me to this incredible, good-looking guy named Jimmy Seibert. We began dating through this journey of my recovery, and after a year and a half he asked me to be his wife.

Six months into our engagement and two months before Jimmy and I were to get married, I was sitting in church when the pastor began to close the service. Suddenly, he stopped and said he felt the Holy Spirit telling him there was a young lady in the audience who had issues with her father and needed to deal with them before she got married. He warned that if she did not ask for forgiveness and get these issues straight, she would carry those unmet expectations into her marriage. I had never even met the pastor, but I knew he was talking about me.

My stomach twisted with butterflies, and I knew I had to respond. I took that word seriously and began to deal with my heart. I started the process of forgiving my dad by setting him free from my unrealistic expectations. He had done his best to raise me, and it was time to let him off the hook and move on. This act of obedience would be even more of a springboard to my wholeness.

It was that moment in church that awakened me to how deeply I still needed healing. This event opened my eyes to the fact that I was on an unending journey of letting the Holy Spirit search my heart and heal my brokenness. King David in Psalm 139:23-24 prays, "Search me, O God, and know my heart; try me and know my anxious thoughts; and see if there be any hurtful way in me, and lead me in the everlasting way." Taking ownership of my unforgiveness would allow Jesus to fully heal my heart and begin to bring the full life that He brings to those who love Him and follow Him. Jesus went to the cross not only to deliver me, but also to give me an abundant life. And forgiveness was the key.

My anorexia was a catalyst to understanding my great need for a Healer. I am thankful that as I began to identify more with who God says I am than what I had experienced, or thought of myself, the more whole I became as a person. Letting God heal me from the past and embracing who I am in Christ has been key in helping me lay solid foundations for my own children and create structures and guidelines to help them become confident, loving, overcoming adults.

JIMMY

I grew up in a fairly dysfunctional family. My mom had come from a broken home, and out of her hurt she struggled with control, fear, and anger. My dad was a peaceful man, but passive. The way things worked in our home was that mom ran the show with her own brand of unintentional control while dad tried to keep peace. I believe they both did their best to provide for us and love us, but I still found myself with unmet needs in my life.

My home was not a refuge. So from a young age, I set out in search of things to make me happy: friends, drinking, girls. It didn't matter, as long as I fit in. As long as I was liked, I was game. Before I accepted Jesus at age seventeen, my life was consumed with these empty pursuits.

Thankfully, my college years became a time of restoration.
As Jesus made Himself real to me, I found freedom from
past relational issues; I forgave my mom; and I finally established a Christ-centered worldview for my life. Without a
doubt, these years set a firm foundation for marriage and parenting. If I had not experienced this transformation, I would
have continued to live out of my brokenness, even though I
was saved, and I would have ultimately brought the past hurt
into my new family. My spiritual wholeness was an essential
foundation for my calling as a parent.

Some of you resonate with our family background; many of
you have faced much worse; some of you came from healthier
homes. Regardless, we all need healing. We all need a work of
restoration. No parenting tips will fix your past brokenness.
We all need to look inward first and let the Holy Spirit transform our hearts. If you want to parent without regret, that is
where you start.

OUR STEPS TO RESTORATION

Healing begins with *receiving forgiveness*. Laura and I both
had places of guilt and shame that needed cleansing. During
our college years, we learned to confess our sin to both Jesus and to other believers. 1 John 1:9 says, "If we confess our
sins, He is faithful and righteous to forgive us our sins and to
cleanse us from all unrighteousness." Through confessing sin
and receiving His forgiveness, we found freedom to live a new
life. We resolved that no past sin would keep us from a bright
future. We were honest with God and honest with one another
to put everything from the past on the table and let His grace
set us free. Every person has places of guilt and shame. And
nothing surprises God. His Word tells us that "while we were

yet sinners, Christ died for us" (Romans 5:8). It is by being honest with Jesus about our sin that we are cleansed, forgiven, and accepted.

Next comes the act of *extending forgiveness*. Forgiving those who hurt you is difficult, especially when the wound came from the very parents who were supposed to care for you the most. Parents have such a powerful influence over their children that their failures, though sometimes minor, can hurt deeply. For some, the pain is so great it feels impossible to let it go. But through the grace of God we can let what feels impossible become possible. And it's only through forgiveness that we truly deal with the pain.

Jesus modeled real forgiveness. He was betrayed by those He loved, falsely accused by those He served, and abandoned by His closest friends. But on the cross, before His last breath, He looked at those who had crucified Him and said, "Father, forgive them; for they do not know what they are doing" (Luke 23:34).

Our parents tried their best to raise us and love us, but at times their own brokenness didn't allow them to see what they were doing. Laura and I knew that only by forgiving them would we truly be set free from the pain we felt. Without forgiveness we would still be trapped and ultimately set up to repeat the same mistakes.

I went back and forgave my mom for every hurtful thing she had done. I also asked her to forgive me for every way I had been vengeful and hurtful. I did not demand that she take responsibility for her actions; however, I did need to take responsibility for mine. Forgiveness is freedom for both you and the one who hurt you. And ultimately, forgiveness is the freedom for your family to truly have a fresh start.

ESTABLISHING A BIBLICAL WORLDVIEW

Throughout our dating process I was always more into our relationship than Laura. I am passionate and quick to act, but Laura is a cautious decision-maker and, once resolved, loyal to the end. Before getting married, we recognized we needed to learn how to make decisions together.

Our journey of personal wholeness revealed how much of our perspective was shaped by the secular world. We realized that in order to make godly decisions for our future family, we first needed a godly worldview. We needed a firm commitment that Jesus and His Word would be the center of all our decisions, even if it meant being uncomfortable. Marriage couldn't just be about pleasing ourselves, or even each other; it had to be about pleasing God.

Before our engagement, we made the following resolution: "If we agree to marry then we agree to obey God the rest of our lives, no matter what. Regardless of whether you like it or I like it, or whether your parents or my parents support our decisions, or whether our friends come along with us, we agree that we will love and obey Jesus and His Word from here on out." Of course we sought counsel from both our friends and our parents for their thoughts and input on decisions we were making, but overall we resolved that whatever God called us to do, He would have the final say.

THE POWER OF MARRIAGE

When Laura and I were sure that God had called us to be married, we also resolved in our hearts that divorce was not an option. We resolved that our lives were no longer our own and we belonged to one another. We believed with all of our hearts that the power of a covenant to one another would keep us through the ups and the downs of married life. Whenever that solid commitment is made, it creates a safety net for your children now and in the future. Most children are asking not just "Who am I?" but "Whose am I?" When they see that Mom and Dad are committed wholeheartedly to them and to one another, it provides an environment of security and peace they cannot find anywhere else.

Marriage is difficult. Laura and I would be the first to say that we have had great days of flourishing and days of struggle. No matter the situation, our commitment has been to draw to one another and not away from one another. We resolved to work through our differences and conflicts, not just because of our love for one another, but also because of our love for our children. In their growing up years, our kids knew that every Thursday night was Mom and Dad's date night. This was our time to reconnect with each other and let the kids know that our marriage was a priority. They were not always romantic or perfect, but these consistent dates kept us connected to one another.

THE POWER OF AGREEMENT

Laura and I not only were committed to our own relationship as a place of security and protection for our kids, but we were also committed to finding places of agreement in leading, training, and disciplining our children. We would spend time getting feedback from other families, dialoguing about issues together and praying together for wisdom when we didn't know what to do. Laura and I agree that though we have struggled at times in our marriage, we have found a place of great strength and agreement in parenting our kids.

We have found that many people tend to parent out of what they saw was wrong in their own families. Sometimes we are too loose with our kids because we were raised too strictly. Sometimes we are too strict because we have fears that our kids will turn out too wild. Whatever your past is, there has to be an agreement in marriage to not react to the past, but to lay a healthy path to the future. As Laura and I communicated earlier in this chapter, it was our biblical commitment that would lay the foundation for how we would see life and do life together. Our kids have not played one of us against the other because we decided early on we would not allow this. Instead, we are intentional about being on the same page before we make decisions. When kids see their mom and dad parenting together, it produces consistency and order in the home.

Parenting from wholeness is foundational to parenting without regret. Jesus is more committed to us than we could ever imagine, and He is more committed to our kids than we could ever be. Regardless of whether you are just beginning or are already far down the road in the journey of parenting, allow God to heal and restore your heart. Then take the hands of your spouse, or if you find yourself alone take the hand of God and agree that you will do it His way. We believe this commitment will set you up to walk in His power and wisdom for whatever your kids need.

"As kids, we knew we were Mom and Dad's top priority. The order in the house was Jesus, family, and then ministry. I knew Dad and Mom would drop anything for us if we needed them to. Though Dad was busy and traveled, he always started and ended the day with us. Growing up, Dad led family devotions each morning and helped Mom get us out the door. When bedtime came around, Mom and Dad would stop whatever they were doing to tuck us in bed, sing us a goodnight song, and pray for us. And when Dad traveled, we woke up and watched a recorded video he had left for each day he was gone and stayed up for the goodnight phone call to hear his voice from a phone booth thousands of miles away."

LAUREN

2

THE VALUE OF CHILDREN

Behold, children are a gift of the LORD.
Psalm 127:3

LAURA

I was twelve years old when I had my first chance to babysit. My neighbor asked if I could watch her infant for a few hours while she went to a meeting. She mentioned it would be during the baby's naptime so it should be really easy. With my mom's assurance that she would be home if I needed her, I accepted the job. Things were great for the first hour as the baby slept peacefully and I read a book in the next room. But then he started to cry. I first tried to settle him down with his pacifier, but that didn't work so I decided to rock him in a chair. When I picked the baby up I realized his diaper was wet.

In the 1970s babies still wore cloth diapers and plastic pants. I knew I had this down, because I had practiced for this occasion by changing baby doll diapers and was confident in my ability. I collected the supplies—diaper and pins, wet washcloth, plastic pants—and started the process. Suddenly, the unpredictable happened: the baby started to squirm. My baby dolls at home didn't move and didn't cry; they always complied when I changed their diapers. But he was moving a lot. As I pinned on the diaper, I accidentally poked him and drew blood. The baby started screaming, and so did I. I called my mom, who quickly swept in to the rescue.

Needless to say, I never babysat again.

As the youngest of three kids from parents who were only children, I had no cousins or younger siblings to look after. This baby thing was completely new to me. In fact, even having children was a miracle for us. When I struggled with anorexia in college, one doctor told me that because of the strain it had placed on my body for so long, I might not ever be able to conceive. I seldom thought of becoming a mom and had little vision for being a parent. The birth of our first child was a major adjustment to the life I had known.

I remember looking at our first daughter, Abby, and thinking, "What in the world do I do now?" I'd been serving beside Jimmy in our ministry training school and having the time of my life helping other girls learn to walk with Jesus. I attended class every day and participated in our regular outreaches. Most of my time was spent with single or newly married women who wanted to change the world through missions.

When Abby was born, I had only one friend who was a mom. In addition, Abby was a very colicky child. She cried constantly, forcing me to leave the school and take her home. I soon found that she demanded all my time and energy. About five months into motherhood I discovered something unsettling.

I didn't like it very much.

Don't get me wrong, I loved my little girl with everything in me, but at the time she felt like a burden that was slowing me down. I wasn't sure how I would ever find fulfillment as a mom. Discouragement settled on me like a tangible weight.

During one especially challenging day I cried out to God, "Is this worth it? Can I even do it? Who am I going to become if I give myself to this parenting thing? She takes all of me, and I need to see the purpose in it."

He answered in the quietness of His voice, "Laura, quit looking around for a different purpose. I have given you this little one to disciple to change the world. Of all the people on the earth, I have chosen you to parent this child. You have what it takes when you lean into Me. I do not intend for you to walk this alone. I am with you. If you give yourself to this journey, you will touch the nations of the earth through your kids. You want fruit? Learn to walk with Me and pour into this child. We will do this together."

Questions flooded my mind: Is this what I wanted? Could I alter my thinking enough to see my role as a mom to be missional, just as important to God's Kingdom as moving overseas to share Jesus with those who had never heard? It was in this moment I realized that if I intentionally invested in the children God gave me, I would discover part of His purpose for my life too. It was my role to help lead my kids into loving God

I may NoT be a perfect Mom, But I am the perfect Mom for Jack & Graham and living for His purposes. This was a critical part of fulfilling His will for my life.

JIMMY

Abby was born three weeks early. Laura hardly had to push. We had just settled down for the long haul when that baby came flying out into the arms of a startled doctor. I leaned over to behold my firstborn and saw a pointy head and a hairless body covered in goo. Nevertheless, at the first sight of her, all I could say was, "She's beautiful. She's beautiful."

Everyone else in the room saw something different. But she wasn't their daughter, she was mine. All I saw was beauty. With the birth of each of our children, I had a similar overwhelming love from the very beginning. As I look back on those moments, I know I was experiencing only a fraction of the love God has for these children. They were His idea. His creation. And we had the privilege to raise them.

Just as Laura and I had committed to having a Christ-centered worldview in our marriage, His Word came alive to us regarding the value of children. To parent without regret we need to see children as Jesus sees them, and that starts by going to the Bible.

CHILDREN ARE MADE IN HIS IMAGE

For You formed my inward parts;
You wove me in my mother's womb.
I will give thanks to You,
for I am fearfully and wonderfully made;
Wonderful are your works,
And my soul knows it very well.
My frame was not hidden from You,
When I was made in secret,

And skillfully wrought in the depths of the earth;
Your eyes have seen my unformed substance;
And in Your book were all written
The days that were ordained for me,
When as yet there was not one of them.
How precious also are Your thoughts to me, O God!
How vast is the sum of them!
Psalm 139:13-17

LAURA

I still remember when the doctor put each of my kids in my arms after they were born. I was completely overwhelmed. It was almost too much for me to think that just moments before, this little life was inside my body. I remember gazing at each hand and foot, counting fingers and toes, amazed at God's perfect design. They each had their own unique personality, their own thought processes, and would one day grow up to be a lawyer, a nurse, a teacher, or a professional athlete. Maybe even the President of the United States.

This passage in Psalm 139 clearly describes how each child is literally put together by God. Stop and think for a minute about the incredible process of a child growing in a mother's womb. Every child is a miracle and is designed to be a blessing both to their parents and to the world.

We were fully convinced of this, but still needed reminding from time to time. When hard days came, which was often, we wondered if our child was really a blessing after all. When a baby who smells less than pleasant is screaming in your arms and refuses to eat, it's not the easiest thing to see them as God sees them. That's when we would go back to God's Word for a reminder. Just a little time in Scripture would renew our perspective and strengthen us to keep on going.

CHILDREN ADD VALUE TO A FAMILY

Behold, children are a gift of the LORD,
The fruit of the womb is a reward.
Like arrows in the hand of a warrior,
So are the children of one's youth.
How blessed is the man whose quiver is full of them;
They will not be ashamed
When they speak with their enemies in the gate.
Psalm 127:3-5

Where there is no vision, the people perish.
Proverbs 29:18, KJV

JIMMY

When we begin the journey of becoming parents, we need to have a clear vision of the importance of family. Throughout history, children have been viewed as a necessary part of the household. In earlier days they were needed to help clean and cook, plant the garden or the field, and ultimately grow up to provide leadership for the family to flourish and survive.

As our culture has grown in affluence, so has our sense of individualism. In turn, many have lost a vision for the power of family. I grew up with several Jewish friends. I loved to be at their houses because there was such a sense of family and commitment to one another. I also knew when I competed against one of my Jewish friends in sports that his entire family was altogether against me. They knew who they were together, not just individually, and supported one another in everything.

Laura and I realized each child God gave us was a precious individual, but they were also part of a team that would grow together in mission and purpose and love. We would partner together with these kids and work through the ups and downs of life. We would serve one another and learn how to serve at each other's side. When we view our children as valuable parts of a team and not just individuals, we see them as invaluable to our family and to God's greater plan.

CHILDREN ARE OUR GIFT AND REWARD

Each child adds value to our lives. Sometimes we wonder what that value is in the midst of the struggle of helping them find their place in loving and serving as a part of the family. But my experience is that not only has God given you a gift in each of your children, but when they know you view them as a gift, they rise to be who they were called to be.

When our son Caleb was little, he was quite an active guy and constantly needed correction. When he was about six years old he realized he got more correction than all the other kids. He was mad at us and down on himself. One day I sat down with him and let him know that all the energy and fun inside of him were needed in our family, but there was a time and place for it (not all the time and everywhere) and he just needed more help because he was so gifted. Somehow he believed me and would often remind me that he got more correction because he was so gifted. (It worked!) Today he truly is a confident, loving man.

CHILDREN ARE OUR INHERITANCE

When we think about the word "inheritance," we usually imagine a large sum of money passed from one generation to the next. In Scripture, however, an inheritance refers not only to finances, but also to the impact you have on men and women you leave behind, those who will carry your name and values to future generations. God is a generational God, and His intention is that every generation will become better than the one before. Psalm 103:17 says, "But from everlasting to everlasting the LORD'S love is with those who fear him, and his righteousness with their children's children" (NIV).

All of us will leave an inheritance. Our investment in our kids will affect their children's children. The incredible value of raising kids is your greatest way to leave a legacy that can change the world. That's why passing values on to your children—a love for God and for others—is so powerful. Every investment you make has the potential to impact your family long after you are gone from the earth.

CHILDREN TEACH US ABOUT GOD

Truly I say to you, unless you are converted
and become like children,
you will not enter the kingdom of heaven.
Matthew 18:3

God honors the simplicity and faith of children. Jesus repeatedly set children as an example of innocence, purity, and faith. Laura and I realized soon enough we were not only to teach our kids about God, but they were going to teach us about Him as well. All of us are on a journey to understand how much God loves us and cares for us. We often see ourselves when we interact with our kids, and it reveals to us how we see God.

* * * * * *

The year 2001 was a perfect storm of compounding trials. The terrorist attacks on September 11 were horrible enough, but add to that the fact that two of our missionaries and dear friends from church were imprisoned in Afghanistan. For over a month we'd been working around the clock to secure their release, to no avail. When the United States began its bombing campaign over the very city where our friends were held captive, our prayers took on an even greater sense of urgency. One of the imprisoned missionaries, Heather Mercer, had babysat our kids before moving oversees, so the gravity of the situation was very real to our children. As we watched the bombs fall on TV, we cried out to God for their safety and escape.

One night during this same period of time, a series of tornadoes hit the Waco area. I'll never forget hearing the sound of the warning sirens blaring above the roar of the wind. The TV weather radar was so full of warning spots it seemed the entire county was one single blob of red. Tornadoes were beginning to touch down. It was time to take shelter. Right then, eight-year-old Lauren went into hysterics, crying, "Daddy, Daddy, what are we going to do?" I knew she was terrified, not just of the storm, but for our imprisoned friends in grave danger overseas. Suddenly, in the midst of her screaming, the electricity went out and the house went dark. I quickly picked her up while Laura comforted the other kids. Lauren was shaking her head back and forth, crying and screaming.

I tried to get her attention, saying, "Look at me, Lauren, look at me! There is no storm, there is no army, there is no event that is bigger than Jesus. Jesus has us in the palm of His hand. Jesus has Heather and Dayna in the palm of His hand. Jesus has you in the palm of His hand. Your name is written on His hand, and He knows the hairs on your head. We are being carried by Him. Look at me, look at me!" Slowly, as I made her look into my eyes, her crying stopped and I began to speak softly about Jesus' love, about His power, about His great strength and ability to carry us through no matter what may come our way. As I did, she calmed down.

"Sweetie," I said, "just rest your head here on my shoulder, and I will hold you all night long. But you need to know all the more that Jesus is holding you." She quickly fell asleep on my shoulder.

I was overwhelmed by the goodness of God. I was overwhelmed by His power to bring peace to a child. In that moment, I felt Him speak to me as well, "Peace, be still My son, for I am with you, too. Whatever comes your way, whatever trials or challenges—I am big, I am loving, I am kind, and I have you in the palm of My hand."

Years later, Lauren and I look back to that memory and realize it marked us both. It taught us to trust God in the midst of the uncertainties and storms of life. If we stop and watch and listen, God is speaking through the little ones right in front of us.

Your children are not an accident, and parenting is not meant to be a burden. Raising a child is an incredible partnership with the God who created them. Through parenting, we discover His perspective on children, we engage His mission for our life, and ultimately we learn about His love for us. To parent without regret, you need to understand the value of children.

"My parents shaped the way I think about most of life. As an adult it's funny to look back and see my parents' finger-prints on how I do the things I do. They taught me practical things—like how to daily make my bed, exercise, eat healthy, and create and follow a schedule—and things that went to the heart—such as honoring authority and keeping my body holy. Through it all, they taught me that my relationship with Jesus directly influenced both my practical life and my spiritual life, therefore it was to be prized first and foremost. I am who I am today because of their profound influence on how I see and live life."

YOU ARE THE #1 INFLUENCER

Follow my example, as I follow the example of Christ.
1 Corinthians 11:1, NIV

LAURA

My husband laughs at me, but I can't help it. I have a few "quirks" that I picked up from my mom. I want to split everything—a meal, a Coke, a cookie, a donut. I eat sandwiches in two parts or sometimes leave the bread off the top of the sandwich. I cannot even pop a whole peanut M&M into my mouth. I have to bite it in half first.

Okay, so what's wrong with that? That's what my mom did. I didn't think anything of it until my husband told me it was weird. My mom taught me a lot about life, sometimes without her even knowing it.

A few years ago I was sitting with my twenty-year-old daughter in a coffee shop, and she made a very interesting comment: "Mom, today I was putting chocolate candies on my roommate's bed for Valentine's Day, and I said to myself, 'I'm acting like my mom.'"

I felt complimented, and I felt sobered. Whether good or bad or quirky or significant, we will never fully grasp the influence of being a parent. My life deeply impacts my children just as my mother's life impacted me.

JIMMY

I wanted to be just like my dad. I waited for his carpool to drop him off at the corner after work, and I walked by his side all the way home. My dad used a hair gel called Brylcreem to slick his hair back every morning. I remember many times standing in front of the mirror and taking Brylcreem in my hands, slicking my hair back, wondering if I looked just like him.

As was so common for men of his generation, my dad never understood the power of his influence. As a result, he passively slipped into the background as peers became my role models. What if my dad had really known the power and impact he could have had? What if he had known I wanted to be just like him? The early years of my life would have looked far different.

This should be both sobering and exciting for us. You are the primary influencer in the lives of your children. You have the power to take these God-given creations and partner with

Him to form them into the people they are called to become.

How you live matters.

Our words, attitudes, and actions have a greater influence on our kids than we can ever imagine. To parent without regret you must take time to fully understand your influence. It will shape and determine your child's values, worldview, and destiny.

INFLUENCE OF THE FATHER

Both Christian and secular psychologists agree that the father has a unique role in each child's development. Though we will go into depth in the following chapters, let us start by highlighting a few roles fathers play.

Modeling the Heavenly Father

One of the primary ways God is described throughout Scripture is "Father." As a result, much of our understanding of God is connected to our relationship with our earthly father. (No pressure, dad!) It matters to our kids how we model the Father in the way we parent. Our sons will find confidence or insecurity and our daughters will feel beautiful or unwanted based on how we engage them in the journey.

Our Words

After years of pastoral counseling, I have seen that a father's words stick in children's minds and mark them for the rest of their lives. Words like "You sure are beautiful, honey," are life-giving words that bring a girl confidence and security in her maturing years. Others, like "You always mess everything up," follow children like a shadow into their future and take away courage and the ability to risk. Realizing that, I resolved to make the words I spoke words of love and affirmation. I even wanted correction to be done in a way that was not condemning but helpful for change. At times, my words were harsh. In those moments I committed to quickly repent to my children and make things right. Our kids did not expect us to be perfect, but they did need to know we cared.

I coached many of my kids' sports teams for fourteen years. When Caleb was ten years old I coached his soccer team. I missed the first half of a game to officiate a wedding, but after the wedding I drove quickly to the soccer field to catch the second half. I arrived before halftime and saw our team a couple hundred yards away. Caleb had just received the ball at midfield. As I jogged toward the field, I began to shout out directions as I normally would from the sidelines. I yelled to Caleb, "Go down the sideline," and without looking up he ran to the sideline. Then, "Cut to the middle," and he cut to the middle. When I shouted, "Shoot! Shoot!" he instantly drilled one to the back corner of the net, scoring right before the half ended.

After the game (which we won, by the way) I asked, "Caleb, do I embarrass you when I yell like that?"

"No, Dad! I love it. When I hear your voice I am stirred to action."

May it always be.

Our words have such potential. They can be either life-giving catalysts, or hard-to-remove roadblocks to our children's future.

Our Lifestyle

None of us is perfect, or ever will be, but we have to live with the understanding that little eyes are watching us all the time. Our lives are models, be they good, bad, or ugly. Some days I had to apologize to my kids for the way I handled a particular situation or the way I didn't model the life I wanted them to live. Understanding my influence motivated me to make good decisions. Every day can be a teaching moment.

Seibert men are committed to honoring God with our eyes. I've tried to model and encourage us to look away from anything that is sexual, sensual, or inappropriate in any way. This became a normal part of our life, but every so often I am able to get a glimpse of how deeply it affects my sons.

One year our family flew to Germany to attend our organization's international conference. I took my boys, at the time ages eight and four, for a walk to keep us all awake from jet lag. While walking, I felt a sudden tug on my arm.

"Daddy, Daddy," Caleb said. "What are you doing?"

I stopped and said, "What do you mean, buddy?"

"Seibert men look away."

"Look away from what?"

He pointed down the street at a pornographic shop. I was tired and had been looking straight ahead, not seeing anything in particular. I explained to him that though my eyes have drifted before, that was not what I was looking at. And I thanked him for bringing it to my attention.

This moment drove home the reality that my kids were watching my life. From the way I treated my wife to the media choices I made to the way I talked about others, my lifestyle taught them more than words alone ever could.

Our Presence

I once heard a story of a little girl who walked into her parents' bedroom because she was scared during a storm.

"Mommy and Daddy," she said, "can I sleep with you? I'm scared."

"Honey," they replied, "there's nothing to fear. God is with you. Now go back to your room and know God loves you and cares for you." She complied and returned to her room, but just five minutes later a bolt of lightning struck nearby and a loud clap of thunder rattled the house. She ran back to her parents' bedroom and dove in bed between them.

Her parents comforted her, but again said, "Honey, you don't need to be scared. God is with you."

"I know that God is with me," she replied, snuggling between them. "But I need God with skin on. Can I stay with you?"

We as men are called to protect, provide for, and lead our families. We are to model hard work and diligence. But we cannot use our job as an excuse to disengage from our kids. We need to be present as much as possible beyond our work hours. Though Laura was at home during the day with the kids, I knew that once I came home after work I needed to be fully engaged and fully present. For years I had very few hobbies or extra activities because I already had a responsibility I was committed to, and that was raising kids and letting them know they were loved.

I chose to be present when I was home by turning off my phone and not getting on the computer in order to engage in their activities. This is when I taught my kids how to ride a bike, taught my boys to throw a baseball, and played dolls with my girls. Yes, dads, dolls. I'm unashamedly well-versed in the game "Pretty Pretty Princess" on account of how many hours I sat with my girls in their imaginary worlds.

I don't regret a second.

Choosing to be present also gave me time to date my girls consistently. On our dates, Abby, my older daughter, easily talked about everything going on in her life and I barely needed to say anything. I always left those times knowing we had a great connection. However, Lauren, our other daughter, did not talk much when she was little and we often simply sat side by side. I asked her questions, and she gave small but sweet responses. For a while I wasn't sure these dates were making much of a difference in her life. Finally, after one of our dates together, Laura asked her, "How was your date with Daddy?" Lauren said, "Oh, it was wonderful! I just love being with Daddy." When Laura told me about her response it brought me to tears. I realized I didn't have to do or say a lot. She just wanted me beside her.

Dads, you have power on your life. It's been given to you by God. You express that through your words, time, and presence. You will never look back and wish you had worked a little a bit longer or gone on another business trip. But you will regret not being intentionally present with your kids. Choose now to maximize these years and schedule time to be present.

THE INFLUENCE OF MOTHERS

LAURA

Mothers have a unique role to play. We represent the part of God that brings nurture, care, and consistency. We show our kids that God is close and present and model what a woman of God looks like.

Our Nurture and Care

I've always been fascinated by post-game interviews of athletes. We've all seen it before. The MVP leans over the reporter, standing at 6'4", weighing in at 280 pounds, smiling from ear to ear after a victory. The first words that come out of his mouth have nothing to do with the game, or his teammates, or even the fans. He looks right into the camera, waves, and says, "Love you, Mom."

These spontaneous, heartfelt words are directed to the one who stood beside him day in and day out, caring for both physical and emotional needs.

The hugs after the games, and the Band-Aids after the falls all paid off. Kids know there is someone back home who is proud of them no matter the outcome. Just like God! Moms help display how attentive He is to the details in our lives. He comforts us when we are hurting and tends to our needs without fail.

Our Intuitive Pursuit

I cannot count how many times one of my kids got into the car after school and when asked about their day, merely answered, "Good." I would intuitively sense there was something on their mind, or their feelings were hurt. I refused to accept their answer at face value and pursued them to truly understand what was going on. I learned to ask questions like "tell me a high light and a low light of your day", or "if you could do the day over what would you like to see happen?" It was questions like these that gave me a window into their lives and often became powerful times of understanding my kids' world and their needs.

Our Role as Defender and Advocate

There is a common saying, "Don't mess with a mama bear's cubs," which I can validate to be absolutely true. My friends and I often joke about how I can turn from a gracious, soft woman into an angry mama bear if someone hurts or rejects one of my kids.

I'm reminded of a story of one of my closest friends that best illustrates this passion. She and her family were at a soccer game. Her husband was coaching her son's team while she and the rest of the parents were sitting in the stands. Several kids who came to watch their siblings decided to play together behind the bleachers, including my friend's daughter. After a while her daughter ran to her in the stands, crying and telling her mom that a boy pulled on her shirt and threw her down.

My friend immediately turned into a bear. Not really aware of the game the kids were playing, she walked directly to the boy and yelled, "If I ever see you touch my daughter again you're gonna get it!"

Still upset, she marched back to the stands, demanding out loud, "Who are the parents of this boy?" as the boy sheepishly came around the corner behind her.

Once the parents were identified, she proceeded to tell them what their son had done to her daughter. The boy's parents checked on the situation, only to find out the kids were playing football and their son had merely tackled their daughter who had the ball. Embarrassed, my friend apologized to both the boy and the parents for acting so foolishly. I guarantee her daughter will never forget that day. She'll always know her mom is on her side, ready to take on anyone who would dare cause her harm.

Our Lifestyle

We influence our kids by how we live—both good and bad. From the clothes we wear, to what we watch or read, to how we care for others, our girls will follow our lead.

Early in our married years I decided I wasted too much time looking at catalogues and magazines. Not only did they waste my time, but they also created unnecessary desires. So I cut all subscriptions besides a few about world missions. To this day, my girls don't waste time looking at magazines and catalogues. In fact, when my oldest daughter got engaged, someone graciously gave her a *Brides* magazine. Though it was exciting to have a magazine in the house after so many years, we found it overwhelming to go through and decided one was enough. More options usually create more dissatisfaction and indecisiveness.

I love to look cute and be fashionable. However, in a world where fashion is always changing and tends toward immodesty, I sought to model a healthy balance. It was my intention for us all to look cute and trendy but without an obsession with buying clothes or being inappropriate in what we wear. We each held to the boundaries of limiting our shopping to what we needed and making sure the skirts and shorts were not too short or the tops too low. Now that my girls are older and making their own choices without me, they still hold to these principles.

Moms model a lifestyle, and ultimately a thought process, for their kids. This trains them to live in the world but not be "of the world," just as Christ intended.

JIMMY

God created us male and female to partner together in the raising of kids. Laura and I did our best to love our kids in the way that He had uniquely created us. Understanding the power of our influence was key for us in making good choices, not only for their lives but also for our own.

SIDE BY SIDE

Our youngest son, Daniel, plays junior golf, and I get to be his caddy in some of his tournaments. In pro golf this is called "living inside the ropes." Tournaments have a roped-off area for spectators, where fans clap when the players do well and moan when they don't. They can view the game, but they are not allowed to have personal interaction with the players. Living inside the ropes when I caddy allows me to walk side by side with Daniel; it is an exhilarating and incredible experience.

Moms and dads, you're called to be more than a spectator. You are not limited to clapping when they do well and moaning when they don't, simply hoping for the best. You are called to live inside the ropes: carrying the bag, walking side by side, and talking about every shot and every contour of life. When there is a victory WE have a victory, and when there is a loss WE have a loss, but whatever we do, we do it together. And for this I have no regret.

I love the example of Jesus. He didn't just create us, put us on the earth, give us the rules, and hope we make it. He chose to walk through life with us. He lived inside the ropes. We have the unique privilege of doing the same for our children.

"I was sitting in a restaurant in New York on my high school senior trip, listening to some of my classmates, for the first time ever, open up about their parents and childhood. As I sat listening to one friend who had divorced parents and another who was really hurt by his dad, I was overcome with how different my childhood was due to my parents' presence and the way they spoke identity over me. I was truly sobered by the conversation and tearing up with thanksgiving.

"When I arrived back at our hotel, a trip sponsor told me that my dad had sent me a gift and wanted me to get it immediately. I was shocked because at that moment my dad was in Haiti due to the earthquake and our church's relief work there. The sponsor handed me his computer, and I instantly knew what it was. My dad had written me a song as a celebration of my graduation just like he had done for my older sister when she graduated.

"I sat in the hotel hallway weeping as I listened to a song my dad had written about me. The gift of him speaking identity over me, in contrast to my peers' experiences with their parents, was a marking moment in my life."

LAUREN

CHAPTER 4

PLACING IDENTITY ON THEM

Death and life are in the power of the tongue,
and those who love it will eat its fruit.
Proverbs 18:21

JIMMY

Many years ago, I spent an early Saturday morning sitting beside Abby while she watched a Bible video. I found myself thinking about how beautiful she was and how blessed I was to have her by my side. But as the movie played in the background, she interrupted the moment by asking, "Daddy, are you proud of me?"

I was caught off guard. Surely I'd misheard. Most mornings the first thing I said to her was, "Good morning, beautiful," and after I returned from work each day, I would scoop her up in my arms and give her my full attention as she shared about her day.

"Honey, what did you say?" I asked, wanting to make sure I'd heard her right.

"Are you proud of me?"

The fact that she had to ask was a jolt to my heart. Immediately I wondered if I'd done something wrong.

"I am so proud of you, sweetie," I said. "Daddy loves you and always will. No matter what happens you will always be mine, and I am proud to have you as my daughter."

She looked at me and simply said, "OK, Daddy. Can I go play?"

Children are always looking for affirmation; they want to know they are significant. "Look at me!" "Watch me jump!" "Watch me run!" "Listen to me sing!" Their hearts wonder who will give them the love, attention, and significance they long for. That person should be you. Your words, coupled with time and affection, will leave the primary mark of identity on your child.

IMPORTANT WORDS

Words We Spoke First Thing in the Morning

For young girls, it's important they know they are beautiful and loved by their parents. As I said earlier, my first words to them most mornings were, "Hello, beautiful! It's time for a great day!" I affirmed their external beauty, but more importantly, I looked for opportunities throughout the day to encourage what I saw of their internal beauty. When they demonstrated kindness to a friend or a right response to Laura, I would stop and say, "You are so beautiful not just because of your outward appearance but because of who you are on the inside. The inside of you is the most important part of you." These affirmations spoke identity and built confidence in my daughters.

Likewise, I woke my sons most mornings with, "Hello, men of God! It's time to rise up!" Men are called to rise up in the face of passivity and to be counted as godly examples to our world. By speaking to them in this way, I set a thought process in their minds to give them confidence that they are not to shrink back from the challenges of life but to take them on wholeheartedly.

Parents mark kids from the earliest age with words. What would God lead you to speak over your children every day in order to impart identity and call them to mission?

"You Are My Favorite."

Every child is put into a family so they can be significant to someone. Laura and I reinforced their identity by telling each child, at every age, they were our favorite. "Daniel, you're my favorite six-year-old in all the world." "Caleb, of all the ten-year-olds in the world, there is no one I believe in more than you." "Lauren, I have been thinking about all the twelve-year-olds in the world, and you outshine them all." "Abby, you are the most beautiful fourteen-year-old on the planet." We spoke these words because we wanted them to know they were significant, wanted, and unique.

When the angel appeared to Mary in Luke 1:28 and said, "Greetings, favored one!" she was shocked. How could God call her favored when she was a simple, imperfect girl? God affirmed His unique love for her while He also called her to a radical mission. When we put value on our kids, it empowers them to believe they don't need to be perfect and they have something to offer the world.

1 John 4:19 says, "We love, because He first loved us." Consistently shower your kids with love and acceptance. This models the grace of God to them and frees them to easily receive His love.

For a while, each of my children felt a little squeamish when I said he or she was my favorite. Eventually they got used to it and it would always bring a smile to their face. Our youngest, Daniel, got so used to it he would say, "I know, Dad," and confidently walk off. Everybody needs to know they have value.

Truth Versus Lies

You will know the truth, and the truth will make you free.
John 8:32

Like all of us, our kids are bombarded with lies about God and about themselves. The biggest way we help them is through keeping open lines of communication to talk through their fears and questions. Our words become truth to them in the midst of their insecurities.

Junior/Senior Prom was fast approaching and Abby, a junior at the time, did not get asked to the prom. A few days before the dance she came home with the reality that she would not be going with a date. It's moments like this that your heart breaks as a parent. We saw the questions rolling in her mind. Questions like "Am I pretty enough?" Or "Will someone ever want to date me?" We, as her parents, knew that we had to speak truth to her over those lies. So I had her sit in my lap and told her that I was not going to let any squirrely, high school boy label her identity. She was the best catch in the city, and they were stupid. I then made her repeat after me, "High school is stupid. I am loved by my family. I am loved by God, and He has great plans for me." I reaffirmed that she is a beautiful girl and a total delight to everyone.

LAURA

I also remember this time clearly. As a mom behind the scenes, it was hard to watch. I remember talking with God and asking Him to give me a scripture or a promise I could stand on for her. He lead me to Matthew 6:33-34 where Jesus tells us that if we seek first His kingdom and His righteousness, He will take care of all the things that make us anxious. I clearly felt that He promised He would one day bless her above and beyond what I could ever imagine. And He did! He sent her Kyle, the best catch in the world for her, and he is absolutely above and beyond what we could have ever imagined.

All of our kids will struggle with personal identity in some form, but if we will confidently go back to God and His Word, we can help guide and direct them lovingly through their journey.

When our kids were believing or speaking something about themselves that was not true, we responded by taking time to sit and talk with them. The conversation went something like this: "I'm sorry you feel that way. We felt like that too when we were your age." We then asked, "Do you really think that's true?"

As they shared, we responded by speaking the truth of God's Word over any and every lie. We led them to Scripture and gave them a firm foundation to stand on. Finally, we always ended these conversations by affirming our love for them and assuring them we would stand with them through the process, no matter how challenging.

Your kids are being influenced all day long by the words

and actions of others. This deeply affects their identity. As they grow in their faith, they'll learn to find their value in Jesus and His Word, but this process takes time. In these formative years your words matter more than you know. Affirm your children and speak truth over them so they will not be shaken by the lies of this world.

TIME

We faced an important decision when our younger son, Daniel, entered kindergarten. We had started a church four years before and, to be honest, I was tired. Our oldest three kids were in a wonderful private school I was involved with and loved. The school gave an option for either full-time or part-time classes and we needed to choose which option we wanted for Daniel. Jimmy was supportive with either option, but it was a struggle for me personally, as it would affect me more than him.

At first, I was drawn to the full-time option. It was exciting to think about ministry again, and I was ready for a break during the day, which I hadn't had in years. On the surface it seemed best for Daniel, too. Being alone with Mom all day is not necessarily the best way to meet friends. So when it came to the decision I signed up for full-day kindergarten.

Halfway through the first semester things just didn't seem right. I picked up all four kids at the same time and almost always the older kids demanded the largest share of my attention with their mountains of homework and endless extracurricular activities. Over time, Daniel seemed to grow more and more independent and withdrawn. His responses to me were more out of obeying the rules than from his heart. I didn't feel the closeness to him that I felt with my other kids.

Soon, I started to question whether or not we should make a change. At winter break, I felt nudged by the Holy Spirit that something was wrong and I should look into him going into the half-day kindergarten. But as I weighed the options, I eventually talked myself out of it. It wasn't convenient for me. Plus, I wondered if my concerns stemmed more from a desire to hold onto my baby. Maybe this was my problem. After all, he had the best teacher, some great friends, and he never complained about going.

But as the spring semester progressed, I felt the Holy Spirit once again leading me to change. Something still wasn't right, though it seemed fine on the outside. By the end of that year I knew I had missed it. One day I sensed the Holy Spirit say, "If you don't fix this now, things will just get worse. You don't have Daniel's heart like you want. These primary years are so important. Even if it is not perfect, it is better for him to be with you."

Jimmy and I prayed and we decided to homeschool Daniel through his first-grade year. This was one of the best decisions we have ever made. Though it involved personal sacrifice, I slowed down my life to spend extra time with this little guy, and I believe it laid a foundation for the years to come.

JIMMY

When Caleb was in seventh grade I was coaching his basketball team and we were coming up to the last game of the season. I received a phone call at work inviting me to a reception to meet the president of Iraq. I had a decision to make—do I miss Caleb and the team's last game, or do I take this opportunity of a lifetime?

I thought long and hard and realized I would only be one of many to shake his hand and get a picture. Even though we were working in Iraq, he would probably never see me again. If I went ahead and coached the game, however, I could seize the chance to love and encourage my son and his friends by either celebrating a victory or mourning a defeat. The choice was easy. Leaving a legacy of time and investment in my kids' lives will last far beyond pictures and stories of meeting famous people.

I have a demanding job, but as my grown kids look back, that's not what they remember. Their memories are of the times we spent together, side by side doing life, not me standing on a stage or meeting famous people. Our kids know we love them when we spend time with them.

ATTENTION

When Lauren was in third grade she was in a choir program at school. The little cafeteria was packed with parents and students. Laura was already there in the back, but I walked in right before the program started and was standing in the open doorway on the side. I could see Lauren looking around nervously. She was clearly unsettled. Somehow I knew she was looking for me. I waved to get her attention, and after several attempts she saw me. When she did, a big smile came upon her face, her shoulders relaxed, and she was ready to sing.

We are made to live with the love and presence of God. He is always with us. In your child's formative years, you represent His nearness. Your life says, "I am here for you. You have my attention, and you are loved. You have purpose and a reason for being."

There are countless opportunities competing for your attention—unfinished work, chores at home, texting your friends, checking emails—to name a few. In our connected world it's far too easy to be with your kids without being fully present. Choose to prioritize your best energy for what matters most.

AFFECTION

Therefore if there is any encouragement in Christ, if there is any consolation of love, if there is any fellowship of the Spirit, if any affection and compassion, make my joy complete by being of the same mind, maintaining the same love, united in spirit, intent on one purpose.
Philippians 2:1-2

JIMMY

I grew up in family that did not show much physical affection. As a result, I drifted and sought inappropriate affection in relationships. I knew that I did not want the same for our kids, so, Laura and I committed from the start to hold each child, to hug them, to kiss their little faces and express a lot of affection.

Some psychologists say one way a little girl knows she is a woman is through the appropriate affection of her dad. The same is true for little boys. Healthy affection fills a need they don't even realize is there.

Our girls shared a room their whole growing-up years. At one time, they slept together in a queen-size bed. Some of our best memories were made when I crawled into bed between them to share stories, talk about their day, and pray for them before they fell asleep. Healthy physical affection is crucial in the proper emotional development of our kids.

Parents have a powerful ability to place identity and confidence into their children. Our words, time, attention, and affection will impact them for the rest of their lives. This requires a commitment. It requires stepping past your own insecurity and saying no to countless opportunities, but you will never regret taking time to show your children love and to affirm their identity.

"My Mom and Dad's prayers have always been a help and a strength in everything I have ever done. Every morning before I go to school and every night before I go to bed, they pray over me and for me. They always know what is going on in my life and pray into that. Without them I wouldn't be the man God has called me to be. Just knowing they are praying for me gives me courage for the activities or problems I am facing in the day."

DANIEL

CHAPTER 5

PRAYING FOR YOUR KIDS

Now He was telling them a parable to show that at all times
they ought to pray and not to lose heart.
Luke 18:1

JIMMY

I will never forget the moment we heard the news. Laura had just had an ultrasound of our fourth child, and the doctor invited us to her office to discuss the results.

"His growth is normal," the doctor began, flipping through a chart. "He's turned the right way and most everything looks good. But," she looked up and said the words every parent dreads, "we have a problem."

My stomach tightened with nerves as we learned our unborn son had hundreds of cysts on his brain. All the potential outcomes involved permanent damage. On the way home Laura and I shared our common fears and pain with the news.

We knew we had to cry out to God.

Ever since we'd had our third child, we'd hoped and prayed for a fourth. We believed God wanted us to have another child, one who would be a blessing to the world. After two years of trying to conceive, we had a miscarriage and didn't know if we would be able to have another child. Then, after four years, we finally discovered we were pregnant again with our son Daniel.

We had prayed for this little boy for over four years. Finding out about his physical problem was a shock. How should we respond? What should we do? Immediately, we rallied friends to pray. We found ourselves calling out to God constantly, sometimes every hour, or even minute-by-minute. Our hearts were bonded to this little boy before he was even born. In my mind as I prayed, I pictured God weaving him together in Laura's womb, healing, restoring, and blessing him.

After two months of prayer and waiting, we had another ultrasound. Watching the screen as the technician moved the wand over Laura's pregnant belly, I saw our child's beautiful form in black and white. The curve of his head, the angle of his fingers, the strong beat of his heart. I tried to discern the technician's reaction as she focused in on Daniel's brain. But as always, she was all smiles. We would no doubt learn the results from our doctor soon enough.

When that time finally came, we sat in her office once more and waited with an odd mixture of faith and worry. Either way, whatever happened, we knew God was good and would help us through any challenge. Still, I knew I had never cried out so fervently for anything in my life than the full healing of my little boy.

"Well," the doctor began, with an actual smile on her face, "I don't quite understand how this has happened. But your child's cysts are gone."

Laura and I could hardly contain ourselves. The three of us (including the doctor) rejoiced there in her office for several minutes. The doctor remained perplexed for something she couldn't medically explain, but Laura and I knew exactly what had happened.

God had healed our precious boy!

Before we left, however, the doctor offered a sobering bit of reality. "Just to prepare you, though the cysts are gone, there might still be damage," she said. "We'll only know for sure once he's born."

As his birth approached, we didn't know what complications awaited. But we did know God had prepared us, and we would love our son no matter what.

When the day came for Daniel's birth, he arrived just as beautiful as our other kids had. The difference was that because of previous concerns they whisked him off for a battery of tests that lasted a couple of hours. We waited in our hospital room, listening to worship music, praying, and contending for our child. Finally the results came back: He was healthy! God had completely restored our son.

Even though we prayed for healing, Laura and I had prepared ourselves for either outcome. If there had been complications, our prayers for healing would have turned into prayers of grace for the journey.

Prayer is how we partner with God to see His power

released in our children's lives. This situation was life and death; we were deeply motivated. But regardless of whether we face a life-altering physical problem or an everyday challenge, our need for God's power is the same. Praying over your children is a powerful and unique partnership with God, unlike anything else. Whatever the outcome, our relationship with Him and our love for our children will only grow on the journey.

Laura and I are motivated to pray because we recognize our own limitations. We can love them, feed them, nurture them, listen to them, and create the right environments for them; but in the end only God can transform their hearts. Only God gives power to overcome their challenges, and only God can reveal the purpose and destiny for their lives.

If we depend solely on our own power to raise our children, we will undoubtedly live with regret. Laura and I committed to a lifestyle of prayer because we knew our children ultimately needed God and what He alone can offer. We found it useful to create a variety of systems to keep a consistent prayer life going for our kids. We put the scriptures God gave us for our children on notecards and used them in our quiet times. We went for walks as a couple and spent our time praying for our kids and would often gather with other friends to pray for our families. These are a few practical steps we have taken to consistently pray for our kids and continue to do today.

HOW TO PRAY FOR YOUR KIDS

Many parents desire to pray for their kids but don't really know how. Through our own experience, here are a few suggestions we've found to be powerful.

Know my limitations!

Pray Promises from the Word of God

Scripture is filled with promises for the peo
These promises represent what God intends for
praying these promises over our lives and the lives of our
dren, we are aligning our family with the Word of God. Laura
and I searched the Scriptures to find specific promises for our
children and the blessing that would come to them if we fully
submitted ourselves to Him. Here are some of the promises we
pray daily for our kids:

"But the lovingkindness of the LORD is from everlasting to
everlasting on those who fear Him, and His righteousness
to children's children" (Psalm103:17).

"How blessed is the man who fears the LORD, who greatly
delights in His commandments. His descendants will be
mighty on earth; the generation of the upright will be blessed" (Psalm 112:1-2).

"In the fear of the LORD there is strong confidence, and his
children will have refuge" (Proverbs 14:26).

"All your sons [and daughters] will be taught of the LORD;
and the well-being of your sons [and daughters] will be
great" (Isaiah 54:13, brackets added).

"Let our sons in their youth be as grown-up plants, and
our daughters as corner pillars fashioned as for a palace"
(Psalm 144:12).

These are a just a sample of the many promises we pray on
a rotating basis for our children. Because many of these prom-

ises have conditions attached to the blessing, we find when we pray them over our children we must first evaluate our own lives to make sure we are right with God. When we respond to God, these Scriptures build faith in our hearts that He will do what He says and we can be secure, despite the many challenges that come.

Pray Specific Promises

Before each child was born we asked God for specific promises for his or her life. We were amazed at the unique words He spoke to us about each one and responded by praying it over them. Laura and I brought these promises before God on a daily basis.

LAURA

When I was pregnant with Abby, we felt God gave us the Scripture Isaiah 49:6: "It is too small a thing that You should be My Servant to raise up the tribes of Jacob and to restore the preserved ones of Israel; I will also make You a light of the nations so that My salvation may reach to the end of the earth." This Scripture spoke to us that she would have the heart of a servant and would be called to serve people of other nations.

This promise gave us great expectation for her life. The only problem was that her personality in her younger years seemed exactly opposite of what God had spoken. We began questioning if we had heard God incorrectly about her being a servant and wondered if we would all end up serving her! She had a strong will and frequent tantrums, but we persisted in praying the promise over her life and committed to lovingly discipline her.

Then something happened that changed everything. Almost overnight her strong will and stubbornness seemed to fade away. What happened exactly? She gave her life to Jesus.

Her salvation transformed her into a servant-hearted little girl with concern for others. When she finished high school, we were not surprised that she was given the highest award for servanthood and leadership, and she chose nursing as her vocation. At the writing of this book, she and her husband Kyle are joyfully loving and serving Jesus in Japan.

We have promises for each of our children that we consistently pray over them. It gives us faith for when they are struggling and joy when we see these promises at work in their lives.

JIMMY

Pray by Listening to God

My sheep hear My voice, and I know them, and they follow Me.
John 10:27

We have big promises to pray over our kids, but daily life is still a challenge. Thankfully, God is with us in the challenge; He wants to lead us like a shepherd through each day, but we need to listen for His voice. We choose to seek Him daily to give us wisdom and insight for what the day might hold. After praying for our children in the morning, Laura and I would sit quietly together and ask, "God, is there anything we need to know?" *pause + ask this!*

Sometimes a Scripture would come to mind, while other times we were simply reminded we forgot to do something we told them we would do. Sometimes God revealed something more significant, such as a deep heart conversation needed with a child or a place we needed to do a better job in leading them. The Bible says in James 1:5, "But if any of you lacks wisdom, let him ask of God, who gives to all generously and without reproach, and it will be given to him." We always found this to be true, if we would take time to listen.

When Abby was three years old, she was quite sick and her fever had been well over 100 for three straight days. We had prayed but had not seen any change. We were resolved to take her to the doctor the next day.

That evening I stayed up to pray a little longer after everyone had gone to bed, asking God if there was anything I needed to know to help Abby. Immediately a picture came to my mind from our recent Mexico outreach trip. Abby had been on my back in a framed backpack child carrier. A man had walked up, licked his finger, and wiped something across her forehead.

That picture became so vivid in my mind. As I prayed I felt that I needed to go in and pray over her, that whatever happened in that moment, whether it was a sickness transfer or a demonic curse, needed to be broken off her life. I went into her room and prayed over her, breaking whatever curse or sickness had come her way from this man. Within two or three minutes, you could feel her skin becoming cooler. Within fifteen minutes her temperature had returned to normal.

I wish I could say I heard God that clearly for every situation; but what I can say is it has always been our practice to ask God to lead, guide, and direct us through prayer. You can have confidence God wants to give you the insight and wisdom you need because He has given you a unique place in your child's life that no one else in the world has.

Pray with Your Kids

There is an incredible thing that happens when you pray with your kids. Not only do you get the privilege of teaching them how to talk to God about the needs in their lives, but you also get the privilege of seeing answered prayer together.

Laura and I would spend every day praying with our kids.

Often, we would journal specific requests that we were asking for: a neighbor to be saved, a provision that was needed, or a breakthrough in someone's relationship or physical life. We would rejoice together when we would see the answers to those prayers, building both our faith and their faith.

One of the most impactful ways we pray together with our kids about big decisions is what we call the 30-day prayer journal. As all of us have experienced in our personal lives, not only in our parenting, there are so many decisions to make. Our desire as believers is to be confident in those decisions, to sense and to know God's direction and leadership for our lives. Laura and I developed a very practical way to do this.

When Abby was finishing junior high and we were praying with her about which high school to go to, she had four options: the large public school, one of two Christian private schools, or to be homeschooled. All of us were open to whatever the decision was.

We knew at this point in her own maturity and life, she needed to have a sense of God speaking and leading her as much as we did. So, we each took a journal and wrote the four options in the front. We agreed we wouldn't talk about it for 30 days but would pray every day and journal our thoughts on each of the options, trying to get a sense of what God was speaking to us and how He was leading us.

What an incredible journey as we would hear so many different opinions! One day, one of us would talk to someone about the public school option and be stirred to journal something like this: "I met John today, and he talked about how great the public school was and what a great experience it was. Maybe God is speaking." The next day, one of us would meet someone from the private school, and maybe the parent would say, "I can't believe that God gave us such an opportunity to be a part of this school. This is the best experience we have ever had." On another day, someone might say, "I've never regretted homeschooling my kids all the way through high school. They are more prepared and ready for college than their friends."

With all these different voices in our hearts and our minds, we journaled every day. The reason we took 30 days is because there are so many thoughts, so many ideas, so many things that God wants to do in our hearts as we process to hear His voice clearly for His leadership in our lives.

As each of us reviewed the process, and as the days went on, one of our options became more peaceful and clear and seemed more right than the others. By submitting our hearts to His leadership, trusting Him, and working through the challenges, fears, and concerns we had about each decision and journaling day by day, we were able to see a theme of God's leadership and ultimately of God's peace.

After 30 days, we sat down together as a family. We each had a notecard on which we had written what we felt was God's answer, but we hadn't shown the others what we had written. We said on the count of three, flip your card over. When we flipped them, we all had written the same school. Wow! We were excited we had all come to the same conclusion. And boy, would we need it! No school is perfect, and the days when she struggled with her peers or with disappointments, we were all three thankful we had a clear word to stand on.

What a great lesson of learning to pray with your kids and not just for your kids. It began when they were little, and even today we do the 30-day journal for big decisions such as where to go to college or even whom to marry. God is faithful to lead us as His people; but our job is to be a people of prayer, to partner with Him, not just in declaring things, but to listen to His still small voice leading us.

Pray for Their Future

'For I know the plans that I have for you,' declares the LORD,
'plans for welfare and not for calamity to give you a future and
a hope. Then you will call upon Me and come and pray to Me,
and I will listen to you. You will seek Me and find Me when
you search for Me with all your heart. I will be found by you.'
Jeremiah 29:11-14

This is a powerful promise. God has wonderful plans for each of our children. He is partnering with us to see those promises come to pass. Every parent has hopes and dreams for their children, but if we're honest, we also have fears when we think about the future. Praying daily gives us both hope and power to overcome the fears and shape their future.

Our prayers went something like this:

God, we ask that they come to know You at the earliest possible age. Let them be filled with the Holy Spirit and filled with the knowledge of Your will. Lord, would You lead and direct their lives and give them Your wisdom on their vocation and the way You have designed them to serve You and others? We pray for their spouse right now in the name of Jesus. We ask that You would be filling them with the knowledge of Your will for their life and place in their heart a passion for You above all else. Would You work out Your will in their life and prepare their heart to serve You? Protect them from all harm and pour out Your favor on them. We ask that our children would serve Your purposes on the earth and live today in Your perfect will, full of joy and alive in You. Thank You that these things are in agreement with what You have for them. We ask it all in Jesus' name.

By responding with faith, even in the midst of our fears, we partner with God. We are convinced He has a good plan for each one of our children. When you find yourself worried about the future, respond by taking time to pray prayers of faith.

Parenting reveals our fears and insecurities because we realize how many things we cannot control. You cannot parent perfectly through your own strength; and unfortunately, when we try we find it exhausting. Prayer not only involves God and His power in your parenting, but also a place of nearness to God for you in the midst of the struggles. To parent without regret requires a lifestyle of prayer.

"For us, spending time with Jesus was like brushing our teeth. It was just a part of who we were and what we did. To this day, my quiet time is the sweetest thing my parents gave me. Now, my daily time with Jesus is a haven and safe place. When I spend time with Jesus, it feels like home."

CHAPTER 6

CONNECTING YOUR KIDS TO GOD

One thing I have asked from the LORD, that I shall seek:
That I may dwell in the house of the LORD all the days of my
life, To behold the beauty of the LORD
And to meditate in His temple.
Psalm 27:4

When You said, "Seek My face," my heart said to You,
"Your face, O LORD, I shall seek."
Psalm 27:8

JIMMY

I had just come in from a run on the beach during our vacation in Destin, Florida. I'd gotten up a little bit earlier than the rest of the family and was looking forward to another great day together. As I walked into the house, my heart was overwhelmed with thanksgiving. Laura, all of our kids, and our new son-in-law were awake. As I went room to room, I saw each of them meeting with God alone, with their Bibles open, their earphones in, listening to worship music, journaling or praying. As I walked through the house and observed from a distance each of our family members spending time with Jesus to start their day, I realized it had worked.

You see, Laura and I knew the game-changer for our kids' lives would be that they had a personal connection with God on a daily basis and valued their devotional lives more than anything else in the world. Laura and I would not be there for every one of their needs; and as they grew older, we knew we could not take care of all the problems that would arise. But just as we had to learn how to live life from God Himself, we knew the greatest gift we could give our kids was a hunger to be alone with God and a disciplined life to be able to follow through with that desire. Wow! Thank you, Jesus, that "in Your presence is fullness of joy" (Psalm 16:11).

WHY SPENDING TIME WITH JESUS MATTERS

We are all made by God and for God. The beautiful thing about God is that He wants a relationship with us. Like all great relationships, our relationship with God takes time, effort, energy, and a plan. When we begin to meet with God day-by-day, it becomes something we treasure above all else.

God calls King David "a man after My heart" (Acts 13:22). We find throughout the Psalms that David found a secret, a treasure: "One thing I have asked from the LORD, that I shall seek: that I may dwell in the house of the LORD all the days of my life, to behold the beauty of the LORD and to meditate in His temple" (Psalm 27:4). David's secret? He wanted to be with God more than anything else. Through his victories, his failures, and his disappointments, he had a refuge: meeting with God, face to face.

We will face many challenges, but God will be with us. What's more, He has designed us to be dependent upon Him for His wisdom to overcome those challenges. A rich relationship with God is an incredible treasure; it will last for eternity. Modeling that dependence on God is the greatest inheritance you can leave your children.

CONNECTING TO JESUS DAILY IS OUR NUMBER-ONE PRIORITY

LAURA

It starts with us. Before an airplane takes off, the flight attendant will give instructions for what to do if the cabin pressure drops. They always say, "In case of cabin pressure change, your oxygen mask will drop from the compartment over your head. Please put on your mask and tighten the strings on the side. Be aware that even though oxygen is flowing, the bag may not inflate. If you are traveling with small children, secure your mask first, and then the child's." This is important because if the adult does not have steady oxygen first, they will pass out and be unable to help their children.

In the same way, we need to be connected to Jesus in order to help our kids. Jimmy and I resolved to not ask our kids to do anything we were not doing ourselves. Before I became a parent I developed the habit of spending time with Jesus first thing in the morning every day. But kids changed everything.

I remember the shock after we had Abby. My morning routine suddenly changed. We were up throughout the night and busy during the day. It felt impossible to get up before my daughter to have time for my devotions. Despite the struggle, I knew that to make it, to be a good mom, and keep my priorities straight I had to find time to be alone with God.

Jimmy and I came up with a plan that gave me time with God in the morning before he left for work. I had a consistent wake-up time, and if Abby woke before my hour was over, he was there to help with her so I could finish my quiet time. If I found I needed more time, later in the day I put her in the stroller and went for a walk to pray and worship.

When we had another child and Jimmy started traveling more, we developed a new plan. A friend made it possible for me to join a private gym. The lady who ran the babysitting was someone I trusted to care for my children (at least for an hour), and I learned to read my Bible and pray while on a treadmill. With each season we continued to make the adjustments necessary to keep time with God a top priority.

It begins with us, Mom and Dad. We did whatever it took to get time with Jesus and then trained our kids to do the same.

MODELING SIDE BY SIDE

JIMMY

One of my sweetest memories is walking downstairs and seeing Laura with a Bible open and a girl on each side of her while she taught them to spend time with God. Each of our kids later described this experience as pivotal for their walk with God. They learned to spend time with Jesus side by side with us before they learned to spend time alone. This is how Jesus taught His disciples.

*GET a Journal
*GET animated Bible

Here is how we helped each of our children engage with God on a daily basis through the Word, worship, and prayer.

Ages 1-5: Establishing Good Habits

At this age you should be helping your children to establish the habit of meeting with Jesus daily. Kids love routine; it makes them feel secure. Blocking off time at the beginning of every day to meet with Jesus creates a normal lifestyle for your child. It is important to communicate that the reason we spend time with Jesus is because we love Him and He loves us. And we spend time with people we love.

At two years old we started teaching them how to have their own devotional time. We sang a simple worship song, read the Bible to them, and had them pray for Mommy or Daddy, a friend, or a missionary. We ended by taking a moment to ask, "Is there anything Jesus wants to say to us?" Then we wrote their response in their journal. Some were quite funny and some were profound.

Our time together was simple, and it became our daily routine. After this time together, which only took five to ten minutes, they watched a twenty-minute video of animated Bible stories, which affectionately became known as the "Jesus" videos, which also gave Mom time to do some other things.

When they learned to read, we bought each of them a new children's Bible with pictures and illustrations, a Playskool cassette recorder to listen to worship songs, and a little journal to draw pictures of what they felt God was speaking to them.

Ages 6-10: Engaging and Connecting

This season is all about engaging and connecting. We helped our kids find worship songs to help them connect with God. We helped them find reading plans to allow them to read consistently through the whole Bible. Reading through the Bible gave them an understanding of God's heart for them and it also created a structure to keep them focused. At this age they learned to pray for their school friends who did not know Jesus, for family members who were hurting, and their own personal needs. Soon they began watching God answer their prayers, not just our prayers.

Memorizing Scripture became a normal part of their lives. We encouraged them to memorize Scripture relevant to what they were going through, and we also chose a Scripture to memorize as a family. We consistently checked in with them to make sure they were continuing to grow. This devotional time normally took ten to twenty minutes a day.

Ages 11-13: Taking Ownership

This is when they take ownership. We asked them how much time they needed to spend with God in order to feel connected to Him. They began to lead the process of choosing Scriptures to memorize, the people they prayed for, and the journal they kept. We taught them to journal their thoughts and feelings as well as what they sensed they were hearing from God.

When their motivation waned, we helped them understand that all important things in life require discipline. We helped them find Jesus to be a consistent rock when their emotions were up and down.

Though they took ownership, they still needed our help to process their questions about God and His Word and how it applies to their lives. In this ownership stage they are moving from the habit of spending time with Jesus to the personal commitment to follow Jesus. Each of our kids was different, but they typically spent twenty to thirty minutes before school in their devotional time.

Ages 14-18: Coaching and Accountability

These years are about coaching and accountability. At this age it was theirs to own; our role was to check in and give them fresh resources to connect with God. We held them accountable just as one adult would hold another adult accountable for those things that matter most. We treated them as young adults who want to honor Jesus with their lives.

Caleb described a moment when he was an early teenager and asked me for help with his devotional life:

I remember specifically one morning when my dad invited me to be a part of his personal devotional time. He said he would just do what he usually does for his time with God and I could jump in wherever I wanted. He had walked me through spending time with Jesus before, but this was the first time I had ever seen just how raw and real my dad's time with God was to him. I remember sitting there, watching him pace back and forth and cry out for the presence of God. He went through Scriptures about the Father, the Son, and the Holy Spirit and then dug into the Word with a depth I had not experienced before. Finally, he pulled out his prayer list. I remember being floored that he actually prayed for that many people every day and took the time to get specific Scriptures for each one. Those moments, more than anything else, defined the way I see my time with God today. Dad was just as raw and real and vulnerable with Jesus with me present as he would have been without me there. I remember longing for depth in my time with God in the way my dad had it. That moment would mark a movement in my heart toward intimacy with Jesus I had not experienced before.

Establishing and modeling your own devotional life is one of the most powerful things you can give your kids.

DEVOTION AS A LIFESTYLE

We all have the same amount of time in a day. How we use it is based upon our priorities. Laura and I determined early on that our time with Jesus would be the centerpiece of our lives. So we ordered everything around our devotional time—when we went to bed, when we woke up, and how we supported each other to have consistent time alone. We did the same with our kids. No matter where we were or what we were doing, the first thing we did every day was spend time with Jesus, whether on weekends or traveling or on vacation.

For several years we took an annual Thanksgiving trip to our family reunion in Nashville, Tennessee. It was a 14-hour drive with four kids in a minivan. We left Waco early, carrying sleepy kids out to the van at 4:00 a.m. The kids woke by 8:00 a.m., so we stopped at McDonald's, ate breakfast, and had a family devotion in the restaurant. One of our kids was always selected to leave a gospel tract in the bathroom, and then we were off again. The next hour was the most important, though, as we had everyone spend time with Jesus to start the day. No matter their age, this was quiet time. The little ones watched their Jesus video and finished by looking at books and listening to worship music. The rest of us used our time in the Word, worship, and prayer. Of course it was a journey to get everyone in sync, but because we resolved this was the most important part of the day, it became normal and eventually a firm foundation for everything we wanted to build as a family. Looking back, these little decisions were the greatest treasures we gave our kids to be successful in life.

There are only a few things that are really important, only a few things that will truly last, and nothing matters more than our relationship with Jesus. If you teach your children how to connect with God, not only will you have no regret, but neither will they.

"My memories of growing up are of days filled with loving Jesus and including Him in all our actions and conversations. It wasn't just about set times of devotions or church, it was a lifestyle. For example, on family vacations when we pulled up at a gas station, Dad would hand us all a tract and say, 'Alright, let's each give our tract away before we get back in the car!' It wasn't a forced thing. We just all knew we were a family that shared the gospel everywhere we went! Depending on our courage and confidence we would hand it to someone, give it to the cashier, or leave it on the bathroom sink for someone to hopefully read. Vacations, soccer games, basketball tournaments, school events—it was all the same. Look for someone to have an intentional conversation with and give away the love of Jesus."

LAUREN

7

TEACHING THEM TO FOLLOW JESUS ALONG THE WAY

These words, which I am commanding you today, shall be on your heart. You shall teach them diligently to your sons and shall talk of them when you sit in your house and when you walk by the way and when you lie down and when you rise up.

Deuteronomy 6:6-7

LAURA

The week was getting off to a bad start.

The kids were irritated, getting into each other's space. If I wasn't playing referee to settle disputes, I was juggling schedules, expectations, and an endless list of demands.

It's safe to say I was getting a tad cranky. And my parenting had become less than joyful.

When our days looked like this, I knew our priorities were out of order. Somewhere along the way we'd lost vision for what really mattered, from simple kindness to one another to the big picture of following God's plan for our lives. I knew I needed to respond by stepping out of the current chaos to regain fresh perspective in our home.

We needed to get outside of ourselves.

After picking up the kids from school, I had an idea of how to get everyone outward-focused. One of the kids' classmates had just had a baby sibling die at birth. It was really hard for the family and the children at the school. Before going home I drove us to a local dollar store. Pulling into the parking lot, I said, "We're going to love on this family, kids. Let's pray and ask God what we can buy to bless our friend."

This exercise can be challenging for some people. Hearing God requires time and an element of risk. What if you don't hear anything? What if you "miss it"? We've found practicing the simple act of listening to God is a great way to involve Him in everyday life. It shows kids how to depend on Him in their decisions. Just remember no one is perfect. It doesn't always work exactly as you'd hoped. But at least you're modeling practical dependence on the Holy Spirit.

We waited for a moment, and then I asked what everyone had heard. One of my kids, who often had a hard time hearing God, spoke up and said, "I saw a smiley face."

"Oh, boy," I thought, "this is going to be hard to find. But here we go, God."

We entered the store and set out to find something, anything with a smiley face on it. Within minutes, the one who saw the picture spotted a purple pillow in the shape of a star with a yellow smiley face stitched on its face.

"This is it. This is what I want to get," he said.

We bought the pillow and wrapped it up with a little note saying, "We saw this and felt like we heard God say He is smiling at you."

We gave it to her the next day at school and left it at that.

The next day I got a note from the mom telling me the pillow meant so much to her daughter. She was thankful we were thinking of her, but the gift itself was deeply meaningful. Purple was her daughter's favorite color, and she had been asking God to let her know He was happy with her. It was hard for her to understand her little sister's passing. Deep down, she felt God might be displeased with her.

The gift was a sign of God's love.

The atmosphere shifted in our home almost at once. The kids were kinder. I even had an influx of joy that refueled me. I found I was more aware of the needs of others and spent more time talking to God about ways I could bless them. Unfortunately, these moments don't last long. I wish I lived this way all the time, but they still remind me what is truly important.

When you're on a mission trip, it's easy to live with a focus on God. But in the normal flow of life, with all its soccer games and carpools and driving all over town, not so much. That's why we've tried our best to use everyday experiences to draw our kids closer to Jesus and help them focus on the needs of others. Living this way makes faith come alive in our kids. It makes it more than a quiet time or a family devotional. Jesus becomes real to them. I believe my role as a parent is to help create environments where my kids can experience the presence of God, and then lead them in reaching out to others. Have I been perfect? No way! But I've tried my hardest to be intentional with the days we've had.

Let's be perfectly clear, though. Most of our days we don't sit around all day reading the Bible and doing devotions with our kids. We've got a house to clean, errands to run, a seemingly unlimited amount of activities to cart our kids to and from, doctor appointments, heavy workloads, and who knows how many other things I'm not able to recall at the moment—maybe I've blocked them out! Life is crazy. Simple as that. I'm sure it is for you, too. Just remember, whatever the day holds, make the most of every moment with your kids.

TIME IN THE MINIVAN

Over the years, we've spent a lot of time in the minivan. I used to jokingly say I was going to hang pictures there instead of the house because it was where I spent most of my time. One day at the dentist's office I was filling out a form for one of the kids' appointments. On the line asking my occupation I wrote "chauffeur."

I am being completely honest. That is what I felt like.

I finally decided if we were going to be in the van so much, I would use that time to connect with Jesus. I took songs we'd been singing in church, taught the kids the lyrics and had us all take turns singing aloud. We also used songs to memorize Scripture. These we played on repeat in order to learn better. I'll admit, many of the Scriptures I know today I learned from songs sung with my kids.

I also used this time to inspire the kids with stories of people God had used to touch the world throughout history. We had an incredible tape series called *Your Story Hour.* These were 30- 60-minute stories of inventors or missionaries used by God to change the world. All of us were captivated by how many life-changing things were invented by people led by God. I emphasized to the kids that these were ordinary people who had an extraordinary God who used them for an incredible purpose.

I would remind each of them they had a similar destiny.

TIME REACHING OUT

Serving others does not come naturally; we all have to be trained to go out of our way to bless other people. When we reach out to others we get our eyes off ourselves. True joy comes from focusing on others instead of living for self.

The few years we homeschooled, we went through a season where we drove once a week for Meals on Wheels. It was not the most convenient thing to load the kids into the car to deliver food to strangers, but I wanted them to see how to care for the elderly. I wanted to show them the power of a smile. Sometimes I encouraged the kids to draw pictures for the people we delivered a meal to. Sometimes we even sang during our visits.

At Christmas we participated in the Angel Tree program and Operation Christmas Child. We went as a family to the store to buy presents for the needy, then wrapped their gifts, put the money in an envelope, and took them to the drop-off station. For several years we helped host the Angel Tree distribution and cooked and served at the banquet for all the families.

We often saw homeless men and women sitting on street corners asking for money. I was never sure what to do in those situations, but it was really hard to drive by and do nothing. Eventually, I came up with a plan to have snacks in the car to hand out when we had an opportunity. (I have to admit the snacks also came in handy when the kids were grumpy.)

We also did our best to share the gospel. We left tracts in bathrooms and with tellers at the bank. We asked the checkers at the grocery store if we could pray for them, looking for any opportunity to share the love of God.

TIME IN THE EVENING

Our evenings were no different. Jimmy usually came home between 5:30 and 6:00 and played with the kids while I got dinner together. He would put aside the phone and email and focus on the kids. At dinner our conversations were catching up on the day and often filled with guests. Our table was a place where each one shared and talked about what God had done in their lives that day or the challenges they had faced (more on this later). The rest of our evenings involved home-work, school activities, or various meetings in our home.

I would wrap up the evening by reading missionary stories and biographies of famous people to the kids. We found a great series of books called Aunt Vera's Bedtime Stories. These were stories of miracles told by a godly woman who ran an orphan-age in Arizona. We ordered the series and read them to our kids every evening for over ten years. They never got tired of hearing them, drifting off to sleep with images in their minds of the goodness and power of God. Every evening we would pray for them, that God would visit them in the night with His love and His counsel.

Overall, my goal was to train them to enjoy God in the midst of everyday life. I wanted their minds to dwell on "what-ever is true, whatever is honorable, whatever is right, whatever is pure, whatever is lovely, whatever is of good repute" (Phi-lippians 4:8). I sought to make reaching out to others normal. Deuteronomy 6:6-9 tells us to teach His ways and commands all day long. While we need structured times of seeking God together, most of our time is spent simply living normal life. Maximize these times to disciple your children. You will not regret it.

"My dad consistently took me on walks and dates growing up, always checking on the status of my heart: How was I? How was my time with Jesus? Was I getting along with my friends? He would emphasize over and over that my little life mattered to him, my Daddy, no matter what boys, teachers, or friends said to me."

ABBY

CHAPTER 8

INTENTIONAL PURSUIT

We love, because He first loved us.
1 John 4:19

JIMMY

When our oldest daughter, Abby, graduated from high school, it was a milestone for our family. After all those years of helping her through the ups and downs of life, here she was, this beautiful grown woman ready to face the world as an adult. I could hardly believe that once upon a time my sweet Abby had been a screaming baby so colicky we could hardly think straight.

It was time to throw a party!

We invited friends and family over to our house in order to encourage Abby as she entered into this next stage of life. As a dad, it brought tears to my eyes to see so many people bringing honor to my daughter.

In the midst of the party, however, I noticed my other daughter, Lauren, lingering at the back of the room. Almost at once I could tell something was wrong. She seemed sad. Soon after she walked over and asked if she could go to her room to finish her homework.

"Is it okay?" she asked. "Since the main part of the night is over?"

"Sure, honey," I said.

As she walked away I knew in my gut Lauren was not okay.

I found my wife among the guests and asked her to take over the party, then followed Lauren back to her room.

"Honey, are you OK?" I asked, closing the door behind me.

As if on cue she answered, "I'm fine, Daddy."

I looked at her face, knowing full well she was not telling the truth. I sat down beside her. "Are you feeling left out?"

For a moment she didn't say a word and just looked at the floor. But then her eyes welled up and tears rolled down her dimpled cheeks.

I put my arm around her and held her close, trying to choose my words carefully. "Sweetie, I know this is Abby's time to be honored. But you have to know we love you just as much as we love her. You're equally valuable in this family."

She continued to cry, leaning against my shoulder. "What are you thinking about?" I asked her.

Through her tears she said, "I was thinking about how wonderful Abby is and how I could never be like her. Do people think I'm as important as she is? Do people think I'm as valuable?"

Okay. Now I knew what was going on.

It was time to speak some truth, clear and simple. "I know it's tough living in Abby's shadow, but as she goes off to college, believe me, you are going to flourish like never before. You are my daughter, just as valuable as Abby, Caleb, and Daniel. You are mine. So don't let the devil lie to you. He's trying to pull you away from your sister, your best friend. He's also trying to pull you away from God's destiny for your life."

We cried together there in her room as we held each other and prayed. It was a poignant moment to say the least.

I'm glad to say Lauren, now a young adult, looks back to this moment as one of the most significant in her life. If no one had pursued her when those lies were going through her mind, then life could have taken a vastly different trajectory. If identity had not been spoken in this time of vulnerable weakness, perhaps she would have wasted years trying to prove to everyone she is worth something. She might have even withdrawn emotionally from the family, which would have caused everyone pain.

Thankfully, she and Abby are still best friends today.

Your kids need you to pursue them. Some moments might seem confusing. You won't always know exactly how to navigate your children's emotions; but if you seek out their hearts, you will be the one they reach out to when things get hard.

Don't wait until they are older to pursue them. We've found even toddlers feel a special bond when we listen to them and hear them out. To do this well we need to prioritize our children and stay attentive to their lives. It's not always easy, but you will never regret winning your child's heart.

MOMMY AND DADDY DATES

A great way to pursue your kids is to "date" them. Set aside time for each parent to go out one-on-one with each child. This creates a time when they know they are uniquely special. Spend time with them to connect and enjoy each other's company. Give your kids the sense that you're safe, someone they can be vulnerable with. If you're not your kids' hero, somebody else will be.

When my girls were little I took them out consistently. We went to the park, rode bikes together, and sat at Wendy's to eat a Frosty and play tic-tac-toe. Simple, consistent time while they are young will set the stage for the even more important times that inevitably come in their teen years.

As my girls grew older and entered adolescence, our dates were spent talking about feelings and helping them understand their true value. We talked about life. We talked about boys. Whatever was on their hearts. It's especially important during these years for dads to show their daughters appropriate affection. Never underestimate the power of a father's hug. Again, if she does not get the affirmation her heart longs for from you, she will find it elsewhere.

As daughters get older, they need their fathers even more. Dads, when you choose to be the main guy in your little girl's life, you'll show her she is valuable, loved, and worth pursuing.

LAURA

I love time with my boys. They wouldn't enjoy sitting one-on-one at a coffee shop, so we spend our time DOING things. We've played video games, lots of cards, board games, and Battleship. We've sat through 3-D superhero movies, sharing popcorn and a Coke; we've walked a lot of golf courses, and we've read aloud together about famous godly sports heroes.

Our oldest, Caleb, has a passion for music, so for one of his birthdays we went on a date to Dallas to see our first Broadway musical. We both liked it so much we made it an annual tradition. Hundreds of hours of viewing sports competitions and eating meals out became my place of deep connection with my guys. I treasure these one-on-one memories with my boys. We didn't always get into deep discussions about life, but we were together. This consistency set the stage for later times when they actually needed to share what was going on internally. We built a heart relationship where they knew they could come to me at any time with anything they needed to talk about.

PURSUE THEM WHEN THEY ARE STRUGGLING

JIMMY

In our fast-paced life it's too easy to take the responses of our kids at face value. When we ask about their day or how they are doing, it's important for us to pause and listen to what is really being said. If they tell you nothing is wrong but you intuitively feel otherwise, keep pressing in until you get to the heart. We often said, "I am going to stay here until we get a chance to talk about what is bothering you."

If you begin connecting with your kids when they're young, they'll want to talk to you when they get older. James 1:19 says, "Be quick to hear, slow to speak." Always listen first; don't lecture. After you listen and hear his or her heart, you can offer appropriate truth. If you only lecture, it's one-way communication, not a relationship.

Many parents are intimidated by pressing in. Some might be unwilling to take the time to listen. But this is often the only way to a child's heart. Remember, your kids long to be pursued by someone, and they need it to be you.

LAURA

It's important to trust the Holy Spirit to speak to us. There were times when the kids left the house and something didn't seem quite right. Maybe I had been too harsh with my words, and they were hurt. Or perhaps they were simply going through something difficult they hadn't shared with me. In these situations I chose to respond immediately, even if it required driving to wherever they were. Multiple times I even drove to their school and checked them out of class to talk. Maybe it was to finish the discussion or merely to say I love you and we can talk about it later. Even if their response was short, I communicated I loved them, was for them, and was committed to working through any relational tension.

Even if you are short on time, your willingness to initiate with them communicates they are worth pursuing. (And a quick text with a couple of happy faces speaks a lot to our kids). Your pursuit creates security in them because they know they are loved.

CONSISTENT PURSUIT

JIMMY

Most Sunday nights, I looked at my calendar for the week and scheduled time to initiate a significant conversation with each of my kids. That may sound a bit extreme, but if I'm not intentional, we will not consistently connect. This is not an elaborate date, just a weekly check-in. It could be a thirty-minute walk around the block or a quick trip to the ice cream shop.

Think of the relationships you treasure. Whether it is your spouse or a close friend, what happens if you never initiate? You can go days or weeks without communicating. Soon things will begin to deteriorate and create distance between you.

Some people resist scheduling because they believe deep conversations should happen in the flow of life. Though this may work for a few, I find the majority of us need to schedule the things we value most.

PURSUIT ON THE MOVE

Life is often a flurry of running errands and traveling from one event to another. Even when together, we are talking on our cell phones while our kids are on their tablets. Our temptation is to not take advantage of those moments together. There are many opportunities to build relational depth in the midst of our daily activities—errands, sports, and car rides—but you have to put the phone down and engage in conversation. When you do, it is always worth it.

When Daniel was nine years old he started to get serious about golf, and I was responsible for taking him to practice every day after work. The course was twenty minutes away; I tried to engage Daniel in conversation during our drive, but he often only gave one-word answers. After getting discouraged about our connection on these drives, I came up with the "3 Questions," much to Daniel's chagrin.

Every time we drove out to the golf course he had to ask me three questions about my life. On the drive back I asked him three questions. The only rule was we had to take three minutes to answer each question. This allowed us to connect at a deeper level and also trained him how to engage others. He may always be an introvert, but he now knows how to carry on a conversation (if he has to).

When I was young, I remember my mom asking me if I wanted her to come to my sporting events. I consistently told her she didn't need to come and I didn't want her to come. My parents often seemed distracted by their own lives, and somehow, even as a little boy I was testing them to see if they really cared. Unfortunately, she agreed to my requests and seldom attended my events. They interpreted my behavior as a sign I didn't care, when in reality, everything in me was crying out for them to pursue me. They took what I said at face value instead of going after my heart. I was a little boy looking for affirmation, and they did not hear my cry. When your kids are brushing you off, even in high school, they're actually saying, "Pursue me. Take a risk. Lay your life down for me. Show me I matter."

The Bible is a beautiful story of God's pursuit of us in the face of our sin. The parable of the prodigal son describes God's heart for His own. He longs to bless His people, and He runs to them, even in their rebellion. In the same way, your kids want to know you will pursue them no matter what.

If you're feeling distance from your kids, pursue them. Ask God for creative questions to get to their hearts. Tell them you notice they've been pulling away, and keep pursuing until you reach a breakthrough. Despite what they might say or do, deep down in their hearts they desperately want to know you care.

"My parents repeatedly said, 'Everyone else may move or leave, but family will always be there for you.' Hanging out with our family was fun and central! Our greatest memories of growing up were being together and having fun with our family. Now that we are older, my parents and siblings are my first go-to. I know they will be there for me, want to listen to me, give advice according to our standards, and pray for me."

LAUREN

CHAPTER 9

FAMILY: FRIENDS FOR LIFE

Behold, how good and how pleasant it is
For brothers [and sisters] to dwell together in unity!
For there the LORD commanded the blessing—life forever.
Psalm 133:1, 3b, brackets added

LAURA

The Seiberts love water. We took every opportunity to take
the kids to a pool, beach, lake, or river. When our oldest was
twelve, some friends let us use their lake house in Arkansas. It
was a simple but gorgeously decorated home on a small lake
with a screened-in back porch overlooking the water. Our days

were full with extended reading, playing games, scrapbooking, fishing, tubing around the lake, and turtle hunting. That's right, turtle hunting. I was obsessed.

A narrow canal led out to the larger lake where the kids could ski or tube. While driving the boat through the canal, Caleb noticed cute little baby turtles all over the bank. They were sunbathing on the warm rocks but jumped in the water as our boat passed. They were so adorable we decided to catch a few.

Catching one was quite an art, requiring teamwork and a closely followed sequence. First, the driver had to be going the right speed. Too fast and the turtles would jump in the lake, too slow and you would never get near one. Second, they had to be spotted. Four of us would stalk the sides of the bank looking for the little creatures. And then we had the catcher, the one being dragged slowly on the tube with the net in their hands, ready to go once one was spotted. We spent hours going back and forth along this little canal, obsessed with our mission. Cheers roared when we actually caught one!

These vacations were just part of the joy and journey of learning to be best friends. The relationships in your family are some of the few that will last a lifetime. Though it requires effort and sacrifice, there is no substitute for raising a family that truly enjoys each other.

VISION FOR BEING BEST FRIENDS

JIMMY

In our ideal world, we have a vision for our whole family to be best friends. Both Laura and I have high school and college friends who have lasted over the years. But as life goes on, as hard as it is to realize, people move away, start their own families, and get busier. We felt the main relationships we could count on in life were with our family.

We've told our children many times, "When the day is done, people come and go, but we always have each other. In our family, we will be best friends."

To this day, our kids feel more comfortable with each other than with anybody else on the planet. Because we valued their relationships, they valued their relationships. Things like daily meals, games, praying for one another, resolving conflicts, and being on mission together created a family that truly enjoys one another.

CREATE SPACE FOR EVERYONE

To be best friends you have to spend consistent time together. At most evening meals everyone was asked to "tell us one thing that happened today that if you didn't tell us we wouldn't know it." That allowed us to hear funny stories, wonderful answers to prayer, and, at times, painful experiences from the day. Having everyone talk (even when they didn't want to) kept us involved in each other's world. It allowed everyone to share what was on their heart. Like most families, some love to talk and can dominate a whole conversation while others are content to sit quietly.

Our daughter Lauren, in her elementary years, was very quiet at our family gatherings compared to the rest of our children. We thought she must be an introvert. One day we received a call from our youth pastor who shared about a recent experience with Lauren. He and his wife drove her to the youth retreat out of town. They asked her a few questions about her life, and she talked for an hour and a half. As they arrived they paused and said, "Lauren, it was such a delight and so fun to hear all your thoughts. We always thought you were more of a quiet type." She said, "Oh no. That's not true. They just never give me a chance at home."

In order to build relational depth for everyone, you need to intentionally create space and opportunity for each family member to share.

RESOLVE CONFLICTS

"Caleb, you're hurting me!"

I can't even tell you how many times I heard this cry over the years. Each time I'd run upstairs and find Daniel pouting in the corner and Caleb defending himself, saying he hadn't done anything. Sometimes he was right and Daniel was just whining, at other times Caleb was the instigator. Regardless of fault, these conflicts always needed to be resolved.

Each of our kids loved being together; but let's face it, at times they drove each other crazy. Our job as parents often morphed into playing referee. When conflict arose, we resolved it. We tried our best to patiently listen and then apply discipline as needed. After correction had been completed, we pulled the kids together to remind them when the day is done we have each other. So loving each other, playing together, and working things out is going to happen. We will be each other's best friends.

We've found that parents often become overwhelmed with conflict between their kids and give up on the hope of resolution. Laura and I determined, by God's grace, we could always work things out by loving, listening, repenting, and providing discipline. Our resolve meant we never allowed conflict to be left unaddressed. This meant hours of talking, often at inconvenient times, but it prevented relational walls from forming in our home. We worked until we returned to a place of love, honor, and joy for our family. Whatever cost we paid was always worth it.

SUPPORT EACH OTHER'S EVENTS

Like many families, during a season of our lives it seemed we were always attending some type of event. Whether something at school, a music recital, a sporting event, or something at church, we lived like nomads in a minivan. Though each child had different interests and different gifts, we made it a priority to support each other. It was not just Mom and Dad's responsibility to show up at these events. The kids needed to support each other in whatever way possible. We did not want any of our children to feel isolated, independent, or alone.

FAMILY NIGHT

LAURA

In addition to daily time together, we set aside one structured night a week that we simply called family night. The goal was an extended and focused time to connect together. These nights also included anyone who was living in our home at the time.

Though we had to adjust for events and school, we consistently set aside a family night every week. Everyone knew they needed to finish homework the night before. We all carved out time for this and made it our priority.

Family night always started with dinner. We gathered around the table and caught up. Then, after a great meal and some good conversation, we did a family activity. This could be playing cards or a board game, doing a craft, watching a movie, going for a bike ride or a walk, or worshipping as a family. Sometimes we used this time to reach out to others who needed encouragement by taking a gift to their house and telling them we loved them.

We had seasonal traditions for family night. In the fall, two or three weeks before Thanksgiving, we bought little pumpkins at the grocery store, drew names, and then had a craft night. Everyone took a pumpkin, and using pipe cleaners, construction paper, markers, beads, and baubles made a likeness of the person whose name they drew. These were displayed proudly on our mantle until after Thanksgiving when Christmas traditions began.

Now don't get me wrong, family night was never perfect. At times we were tired and had bad attitudes. We often wanted to forfeit the time altogether because we were so wiped out. Some nights someone wanted to go to another activity and we had to tell them no, while other nights we were forced to cancel because of events we had to attend. Despite the challenges, we guarded this time.

It was all worth it. Why? Because we were intentional and it showed our kids we were committed to them and wanted them to be committed to each other.

FAMILY VACATIONS

Jimmy and I had the amazing privilege of working with college students when our kids were young. I was always on the lookout for any college student who said they loved their parents and loved their siblings. I wanted to know their secrets so I could have that same type of family. I asked students what one thing their parents did to keep the family close. The students I asked had full lives. Many of them had been athletes in high school, involved in student government, cheerleading, or dance.

I found the common thread to be great family vacations. Jimmy and I took this to heart. We decided our family needed to pull away once a year, alone, to spend quality and quantity time together. This was a time just for us. We spent most of our holidays with extended family, and we always had someone living with us. So we set aside vacations just for us to connect, play, and make memories.

For the first ten years, vacations were not physically refreshing for us as parents, but they were deeply meaningful. No matter where we stayed, the routines still had to be done. The kids still woke up early, needed food, and wanted to be entertained. But it did make for great memories. I think our kids will always remember the books that we read as a family, the many boats we borrowed which then had to be repaired, the girls doing hours of photo sessions, the boys golfing, and the nightly games we played before we went to bed.

Family vacations don't have to be expensive ski trips or Disney World adventures, although those things are nice. We found that being together and keeping it simple has been just as rewarding. One family we know often vacations at home. They turn off their cell phones and emails for five days, and each of the five kids picks one fun activity to do as a family, all within driving distance. They've taken long hikes, read books in the park, gone to a restaurant they had never tried before, and played board games. One kid picked a Star Wars marathon day. That's right, all seven of them spent twelve hours watching Star Wars with breaks for snacks and pizza.

I've also heard of families swapping houses. This way they get to go to a different location and get away from the daily routine and its distractions. Don't let grand ideas and expenses stop you from achieving the purpose of vacation: to get refreshed, to be together, and to make memories that will last a lifetime.

God designed family to be a place of belonging; He intended for it to be a safe place of support where each member is truly known. Live intentionally now to build deep relationships. Choose to prioritize time together over the countless other distractions. Years from now, when all your kids are grown, you will never regret the hours spent building deep friendships. Your investment today will last a lifetime.

"Mom and Dad were always great at putting us around people that were committed to running a family like we were, and this provided a safe place for all of us to grow together. In addition to hanging out with like-minded people, my parents consistently created space for us to encounter God together as families. To this day, my closest friends are the kids from those families. We experienced and participated in the Kingdom of God together, and it built a bond of unity that, at least in my mind, will never be broken."

CALEB

YOUR KIDS AND THEIR FRIENDS

He who walks with wise men will be wise.
Proverbs 13:20

LAURA

We were college pastors when we started to have kids. This required us to spend a lot of time counseling students through the addictions and pains they carried from hanging out with the wrong crowd. We saw firsthand the truth of 1 Corinthians 15:33: "Bad company corrupts good morals." As a result, when we started raising our own children, we committed to doing whatever we could to help them develop positive friendships.

We'd had our fair share of pain caused by sin and rejection from our friends growing up. And it's safe to say we wanted to spare our kids from the pain we experienced. There's no way any parent can control every detail of life, or should even try, but we chose to pay attention to whom our children spent their time with and where they were. This was a significant time investment for us, but sparing our kids the wounds that so deeply affected us was completely worth it.

PROTECT THEM IN THEIR YOUNGER YEARS

In their developmental years, we made sure the friends and families they spent time with were ones we felt good about and shared our values. We seldom left them alone at a home if parents weren't there or if an older sibling was babysitting. We also made sure our kids were comfortable with where they were going. We often asked questions after they had been somewhere about what they did and whom they played with. If they were not comfortable around someone or seemed upset to be left somewhere, we took it seriously and investigated; sometimes their concern was normal separation anxiety, but we also discovered situations we felt were unhealthy.

We changed our plans many times, even declining party invitations, because a child did not feel comfortable. As the kids were still learning our values and developing their own sense of right and wrong, it was our responsibility to keep them safe and away from as many compromising situations as we could. It takes a strong and confident kid to say no to the crowd; while our kids were still developing in their younger years, we tried our best to protect them.

Though most of their time was spent with friends who carried our values, we did reach out to kids living in difficult environments. In those situations, I was focused and present so I could be aware of what was going on. I had a plan for fun things they could do and kept my schedule free to be listening and interactive as needed.

JIMMY

Despite being protective about what homes our kids visited, we still wanted our kids to be social. Our solution was to have kids over to our house. Laura spent hours scheduling and setting aside time for friends to come and play. This prevented our kids from being placed in situations they weren't ready to navigate. Kids need to play and engage with others, but we need to create a healthy place for this to happen.

TRAINING THEIR PLAY

LAURA

Not only were we aware of whom they were playing with, but we tried our best to know *how* they were playing. Often, when they had friends over, I was tempted to spend my time reading a novel, getting my cleaning done, or finishing extra housework. While occasionally I still did those things, I also recognized time with friends as an important training opportunity.

Kids must be trained how to treat others well. They don't, by nature, like to share because, let's face it, kids can be selfish. But if we teach them how to be selfless, how to be hospitable, they can learn how to serve others early on. My job as a mom was to coach them. I expected interruptions, especially when the kids were little. But instead of getting frustrated, I embraced these times as another opportunity to instruct them. Once they were older and I was confident about the way they interacted with their friends, I gradually was able to use this time for other tasks.

INFLUENCE OF SCHOOL FRIENDS

When our kids started to attend school, we often asked them who their classmates were, who they enjoyed, and which friends they wanted to get to know more. Because our kids knew our expectations about behavior, it was easy for them to discern whom we wanted them to hang out with.

When one of our daughters was in the fifth grade she came home upset because some of the girls had started to circle up during recess to talk about boys and who liked whom. They also started to gossip about girls in different classes. This really disturbed my daughter because she knew it was wrong but didn't know what to do besides walk away. After a time, she began to feel isolated.

We felt it was still our role to step into this type of situation. I made an appointment with the teacher and explained what was happening because I knew it was not in line with the school's values. She was suspicious herself and was grateful for the information. In response, she pulled the whole class of girls together and did a life lesson on the meanness of gossip and about not "stirring up love before its time" (Song of Solomon 8:4). I am thankful for godly teachers and that our daughter felt safe to share with us.

We know there comes a time when parents have to stop stepping in to save their kids from every problem. But in the formative years, your kids need to know you're there for them and will do your best to stand beside them in challenging situations. This was a teaching moment for both my girls and the others. Little things like gossip and being mean creep into all relationships and start at a young age. Too often we don't pay attention, or consider such things a normal part of life rather than calling everyone to a higher standard. After all, we are Christians and our calling is to live as Jesus did, not in accordance with what the world thinks is acceptable.

PEER PRESSURE

JIMMY

Peer pressure is powerful. Everyone wants to be loved and fit in; at times I still struggle with that as an adult. But we believe living a "normal" life will not change the world. What everyone views as normal is always in flux, defined more and more by the world and less by God. Anyone who commits to radically following God will feel abnormal.

I often think of Luke 6:26, which says, "Woe to you when all men speak well of you." Jesus calls believers to be salt in this world, and if the salt becomes tasteless, what use is it? (Matthew 5:13) In response, we told our kids to not be surprised if they feel set apart or left out. Rejection for righteousness' sake is hard, but it's the way it's always been.

When Caleb was in the fourth grade, a popular series of books for young readers came out. Kids were devouring them. We felt the content was not appropriate for our kids and didn't match our values, so we told them we were not going to read it. Even the teachers endorsed it because the books were known for their literary content. We didn't make it a big issue with others, but for our own family we drew the line.

One day I visited the school to surprise the kids at lunch. I walked in and saw Caleb sitting by himself, reading a book at the end of the table. Instantly I wondered why he was being rejected.

"Caleb?" I asked, sitting down beside him. "What's going on?"

He closed the book and looked up at me. "All the kids ever talk about now are those books. I don't have anything to say about them, so I decided to just come over and read by myself until they talked about something else."

It broke my heart, but thankfully, he seemed fine. He knew it would blow over eventually and things would be back to normal.

Training your kids to deal with peer pressure is important, even though it may lead to rejection. It requires courage to walk away and be willing to sit alone.

REJECTION

Going into ninth grade can be awkward for anyone. Building relationships was difficult for Abby as she entered high school. She discovered a deep contrast between her classmates' lifestyles and our family values. Even the Christian kids were still trying to decide how they wanted to live. The first few months were heartbreaking for Laura and me because we saw her so lonely and isolated. She had little social interaction with classmates outside of school and few invitations to events. In fact, her friends at school were mostly the teachers. She looked forward to being with her sister and her best friend, Emily, outside of school. It was an emotional struggle to make school a better place for her.

One morning God gave us the phrase, "Go to school to serve and not be served." When you are only looking for others to serve you there will always be days of disappointment. If you go with the opposite attitude, knowing others need love and attention more than you, then you will always find friends because there are always people looking to be loved.

In response, Abby walked the hall and prayed, "God, who needs a word of encouragement today? Who needs a friend? I will go and be that friend." This was the answer for her heart as each day she was able to be a friend to someone who needed her. In fact, when Abby graduated from high school they created a new award that still stands to this day. The Servant

Hearted Award is given to the senior who showed the most Christlike character throughout their school years. We could not have been more proud as parents.

As our grown kids reflect back on those times, they're always thankful. Though it was difficult, rejection did not leave scars because they knew we supported them.

HAVING YOUR KIDS' BACKS

The phone rang at 8:00 on a Friday night. Lauren was ten years old and at a sleepover birthday party. At the time we weren't comfortable with her staying overnight because we did not know the family well but decided she could stay until 10:00 when everything wrapped up for the evening.

As I picked up the phone, Lauren asked, "Daddy, can you do what you told me when you dropped me off?"

"Honey, are they watching something you are not comfortable with?"

"Yes, Daddy."

"Are you uncomfortable with what is going on there?"

"Yes, Daddy."

"OK. Go to Mrs. Jones and tell her your parents' plans changed and we need to pick you up at 8:30."

As we arrived at the house we graciously thanked them for inviting Lauren to the party and apologized for having to pick her up so soon. Later, we explained the situation to the parent and things were fine.

I'm so glad Lauren called that night. It's so important for your kids to know you're willing to pick them up anytime and anywhere. As the years went on, they knew they could always call us; and they knew we would always have their back, no matter what.

We're all made for friendships, but friendships are difficult. You have a powerful opportunity to shape how your children relate to others. Through your investment they can be those who influence their peers for the positive instead of being influenced negatively by others. You'll have no regret in the hours invested in getting to know your kids' friends and helping them to navigate the challenge of relationships.

"People who lived with us became family. They were welcomed at our table, into our lives, our laughter, and our disciplines. It was so impactful to see the ways these young men and women followed Jesus so uniquely and radically with their lives. It gave me more heroes to look up to. Through it, I learned that Christians were not perfect people. They were humans who came in all shapes and sizes with different dreams and ways of pursuing God. I wouldn't trade it for anything!"

CHAPTER 11

THE CHURCH COMMUNITY

And all those who had believed were together and had all
things in common.
Acts 2:44

JIMMY

"Where is Lauren?! Where is Caleb?! Laura, do we have all the kids?!" I shouted over the roar of hundreds of Haitians pushing up against us. "Run! Everybody run to the vans!" Our team of twenty-four along with six Haitian friends jumped into two Toyota 4Runners, hoping we would make it out alive. (No, that is not a typo—thirty people packed into two vehicles.)

We were in the middle of a riot.

It was the summer of 2005, and our family had become great friends with three other families in our church, each of them with four kids. Our children were of similar ages, and, more importantly, we carried the same values. We were trying to raise kids who could not just survive this world but would change it. We knew this meant taking our families to see other parts of the world to engage the mission of God. Everyone took ten days of vacation from work, and after much prayer and planning, we were on our way.

When we landed in Port Au Prince, the capitol city of Haiti, the city was under martial law. But we were able to get out of the city in our rented school bus and head north to the city of Gonaives, where we met the Haitian leaders of the church we would be working with.

What was supposed to be a three-hour ride turned into six. As it got darker and the roads got rougher, I asked myself, "What in the world are we doing out here in the middle of nowhere? Is this right? Should we even be here? Should we be endangering our lives and our kids' lives?"

But God had set us up for a life-changing experience.

We stayed on the church grounds in very simple dormitories. Only two of the small rooms had air conditioners. We congregated in those rooms late into the night before going to our separate rooms to toss and turn in the overwhelming heat. Our meals consisted of ketchup sandwiches, questionable eggs, and mystery meat. We all learned to be thankful for what was placed before us and to do our best to get it down. (We also learned for the future that snacks like granola and peanut butter crackers are not just a luxury, but may turn into survival food).

Our days started in the morning with worship and prayer together, followed by building chicken coops and cleaning up rubble. The afternoons and evenings were spent doing evangelism in the neighborhood followed by church services later at night. Our full day ended with a sweet connection, in one of the air-conditioned rooms, playing games, laughing about our day, and praying for one another.

We trained our kids to lead worship, perform dramas that communicated the gospel, share their personal testimony, lead people to Jesus, and serve people's practical needs. On one particular day we were leading an outreach in the middle of the city. During the drama the person who was playing Satan came out with a black cloak, looking evil, and the crowd began to shout and scream with joy. They were not rooting for Jesus in the drama; they were rooting for the devil.

As the drama concluded, a woman from our team began to preach the gospel through a translator. By now hundreds of people had gathered all around us, and they began to yell and shout. Several people responded to the gospel, but tension began to build between the devil worshippers and those who wanted to follow Jesus. The crowd pressed in all around us.

The kids were ready to hand out balloons and candy, but as they started to give it away the crowd went wild. Both the young and old tried to grab the candy out of our kids' hands. People were pushing and shoving. We were forcefully holding onto our kids so they wouldn't get lost in the growing sea of craziness. In desperation, one of the men on our team threw all of the candy out beyond the crowd, pointed to it, and yelled, "There! It's over there!" This was our window. The mob ran over to the candy, and we fled as fast as we could.

Our team crammed into the vehicles and drove back to the base camp, which was about thirty minutes away. On the ride home we rejoiced and thanked God for His deliverance. The kids thought it was so cool, but the parents could only think about how easily we could have lost a child.

We have committed to living life differently, to train our kids to be on mission. At times we have done "radical things" to keep our eyes and our hearts engaged beyond our American world. We chose to do more than just attend church, we chose to live church; and our lifestyle deeply affected the worldview of our children. The kids from that Haiti trip are all young adults now, and we've remained close through the years. When they reminisce about their childhood, they all point back to events like that trip as the most exciting time in their lives.

Investment in church community, moving beyond mere attendance, built rich friendships and a clear sense of mission for our family. It was a choice, and at times a sacrifice, but it yielded a lifelong return because living on mission with God became our norm.

THE POWER OF A CHURCH COMMUNITY

LAURA

When Abby was born, none of my close friends were moms. It was a challenge for me, and I often felt alone. We were involved in a great church community, but I needed a friend who could help me through all the changes of motherhood.

When Lauren was born, Abby was well into her two-year-old year and started to develop a strong will. I didn't know what to do, so I sought out an older lady in our church.

"I need help," I said. "I need a friend who is in the same stage as me. Do you know anyone around my age who has a strong-willed kid like mine?"

My friend replied, "Call Melissa. She has a three-year-old and one-year-old who are quite a challenge. I'll bet you can glean something from her."

I was desperate, so I called Melissa and went to her house with my two-year-old and my baby. We sat in her kitchen and shared our hearts. I found someone in my same season of life who loved God and wanted to raise a godly family. I realized sometimes just sharing my struggles helped me to process and reach some conclusions. It was reassuring to know she faced similar struggles and that my experiences were a common challenge for moms.

From then on, we decided to do this together as long as we lived in the same city. We committed to be honest and to take on challenges together. We committed to speaking into each other's lives both with encouragement and with correction.

Our goal was to raise children who put Jesus as their first love, were willing to walk the narrow path when no one else was willing, and had a lot of fun along the way. Eventually Jimmy would begin to meet with Danny, Melissa's husband, and we started a small group together. We remain close friends, even twenty-two years later.

Parents, we need each other! We're to take primary responsibility for our children's upbringing, but we cannot do it alone.

After a time, other families were added to our group. We led small group together, went on mission trips together, had sleepovers, cried together, and prayed together. While we consistently built relationships outside these families, this core group of friends was an incredible gift.

You need a healthy church community. You need consistent families to walk with, who will encourage you, challenge you, and inspire you to mission. Many of you are starting like we did, without like-minded friends. Everyone wants a healthy community, but unless someone initiates, it will never happen.

Initiate with someone today; join a small group, and if you can't find a group then start one. Resolve to seek Jesus together. Though it will require sacrifice, you too will see the power of the Church, as God intended.

CHILDREN'S AND YOUTH WORKERS

JIMMY

Parenting is a partnership. Laura and I took the main role in discipling our kids, but we also knew our kids needed the investment of others. These role models gave them a fresh perspective. In elementary school our kids had great children's pastors and volunteers who invested in their lives. They not only met with them on Sundays but also during the week. These activities consisted of lunch at school, after school prayer times, service projects, and in-town mission trips in the summer. As they grew older, junior high and high school youth workers, usually college students, helped them develop their gifts of music, speaking, or serving behind the scenes.

We did everything we could to have other godly people involved in our kids' lives. Our kids have had the opportunity to spend one-on-one time with some amazing people who spoke into their lives. In fact, at Abby's wedding she honored a special group of these ladies she called My Mentors. This group included five ladies who had come alongside her throughout her twenty-two years of life and helped her through the journey to adulthood.

PEOPLE LIVING WITH US

LAURA

After being married for a year, Jimmy and I started a ministry training school within our church. To help with their living expenses, we invited a few students to live with us. We never imagined how much this would shape our family. We loved living in community! Not only were they built-in babysitters and helpers around the house, but they were older "siblings" who loved Jesus.

We found having young adults around the house added other voices in our home who reinforced the character and values we wanted our kids to have. They were eyes for us in areas we did not see well. And in a crazy way, they kept Jimmy and me accountable to respond rightly to each other and to our kids. Let's be honest, it's hard to respond poorly when you have a twenty-two-year-old watching everything you do and how you respond as you parent.

Let me tell you about Stefanie. I was talking to students following our weekly college service when a young woman walked up to me and introduced herself as Stefanie. As we talked, she shared about how she was graduating in May and had committed to our training school the following fall. After a few minutes she surprised me with a bold request.

Though we had just met, she asked to live with our family. We had regularly allowed women to live with our family, but did so only if we knew the person moderately well. This situation was totally different. No one had ever directly asked us before, and I was taken aback.

At the time, my kids were eight, six, and four years old, with one more on the way. It felt like a big change for our family, which made me hesitant, but I committed to pray and seek

God. We also asked the input of others who knew her. The more we prayed the better we felt and eventually agreed.

Stefanie was a gift from God to our family. She practically became a big sister to my kids. She moved into our home with a servant's heart. She joyfully watched the kids for date night and helped me with chores. Stefanie even used her degree in art to teach my kids as part of their homeschooling. She set a wonderful example of trust and purity.

During her two years of living with us, Stefanie modeled for my girls a healthy dating relationship and eventual engagement. While she was with us, Robert, now her husband, began to pursue her. The girls got to observe how to be courted in a fun, healthy, pure, and holy way. Robert won Stefanie's heart by being a great friend, serving her, clarifying his goals and purpose in life, and keeping the relationship totally pure.

Many people were surprised when they heard we allowed young adults to live with us despite the size of our family, but we felt it added richness to our kids' lives we would have otherwise missed.

THE POWER OF FEEDBACK

Walking in community is not always bliss. We experienced incredible benefits, but some of the most valuable were also the most difficult. To experience true community we embraced vulnerability and correction. No one sees life perfectly. From football players to car mirrors, we all have blind spots. Personal growth requires us to acknowledge our weaknesses and to open our hearts up to being challenged by others.

I call this type of community "Proverbs 27:5 Living." The Scripture states, "An open rebuke is better than hidden love!" (NLT). Despite our best efforts and personal response to God, we still need friends to speak into our life and challenge us.

Parenting is one of the most sensitive subjects in the world. It exposes our insecurity and vulnerability, which in turn makes receiving input difficult. We easily become defensive regarding our kids; if we aren't careful, we view correction as a personal attack. Yet, to be the parents we want to be, godly feedback is fundamental.

Don't react negatively when you are given challenging input regarding your kids or your parenting. Even if it was given with the wrong attitude, first go to the Lord and ask for discernment. It is an uncomfortable but small price to pay for the gift of an opportunity to grow. Our blind spots hurt those we love the most and, by definition, we cannot see them without the help of others. Treasure a rebuke from a friend and don't let the pain of vulnerable conversations keep you from the community you desperately need.

JIMMY

Correction can come at times when you least expect it. Robert Herber, the guy who was dating Stefanie, had spent a lot of time at our home. After a few months of hanging around our family I asked him for some feedback.

"Is there anything you see in my parenting or in our children you feel we need to work on?"

He replied without hesitation. "Oh yeah! You get way too frustrated with Caleb."

(As a reminder, Caleb was nine years old and was quite a handful.)

I immediately got defensive. "What are you talking about?" I thought to myself. "You don't even have kids. You don't have to deal with Caleb all day long. I'm actually doing better than most other dads I know with their sons." But, thankfully, I kept my mouth shut and asked a follow-up question. "Robert, could you explain a little bit further? What do you mean?" He shared a couple examples that clearly illustrated his point.

To be honest, I was annoyed. But after he left I realized I was the one who had asked him for feedback. But to make sure that it wasn't just his opinion, I went to other close friends to ask if they had seen the same frustrations in my interactions with Caleb. The verdict was unanimous. I was impatient with my son, and I needed to change.

From that day forward, I committed to change my attitude toward Caleb. It was a process but we worked through our challenges together and today are best friends.

Parents, this type of community is HARD and takes TIME, but it's worth it, believe me. If you are not open to correction then people will quit giving you feedback, and you will miss out on a significant opportunity for personal growth.

We not only opened the door, but initiated feedback from trusted friends, youth leaders, teachers, and sometimes even our kids' friends.

THE DANGER OF ISOLATION

God put us in families, extended families, and close-knit communities because He knew we needed each other. Proverbs 18:1 says, "He who separates himself seeks his own desire, he quarrels against all sound wisdom." Isolation can be tempting to those who are embarrassed by their failure. They want to hide from others out of shame. But this kind of self-protection is truly dangerous.

Isolation also occurs when people think they know what they're doing and don't need any help. Their pride gets the best of them. God has designed for us to walk together with others.

If you feel broken and embarrassed, as difficult as it may seem, run to God's people. And if you think you've got it all together and don't need anyone else, humble yourself and invite others into your life. Proverbs 11:14 says, "Where there is no guidance the people fall, but in abundance of counselors there is victory." You can find safety, guidance, and friendship in community. It may seem daunting to find time to invest in community, but if you are willing to consistently open up your life to others, you will not regret it.

"When it came to sports, I was 100% in. I wanted to do them all, and I had one speed—running. However, for the sanity of my family, we had a rule that we could only play one sport at a time. For my younger years I chose to play soccer. One time I was playing a competitive game with a tennis ball in the house and ended up busting my head on the banister. It was a Friday night, and I got multiple staples in my head. The next morning I had a soccer game that I just could not miss. In my six-year-old mind, I HAD to be there. Eventually my parents agreed I could play and let me wear a sweatband over the staples, but I had a strict rule of no headers. Our whole family packed into the car for the soccer game and cheered me on. I had one of my highest scoring games, and everyone rejoiced. I can only imagine that my mom and sisters were rejoicing that I was not bleeding and still had a smile on my face. This is a small picture of the chaos we all embraced together."

CALEB

CHAPTER 12

ON THE RUN

And Jesus kept increasing in wisdom and stature,
and in favor with God and men.
Luke 2:52

JIMMY

We spent yet another Friday night in line at Taco Bell, buying a ten-pack of burritos and tacos. It was a long week. On Monday night, we dropped Daniel off at soccer practice while we attended a PTA meeting. On Tuesday night, we cheered Caleb on at his basketball game after taking Abby to practice for a play. On Wednesday night, we hosted Lifegroup and sent the kids to youth group. On Thursday night, we attended another soccer practice after driving Lauren to art lessons.

After our family dinner Friday night at Taco Bell, we dropped one kid off at a sleepover while inviting three other kids to our house to be ready for the 8:00 a.m. soccer game and a weekend basketball tournament. After church on Sunday, Laura drove Daniel to a two-day golf tournament a few hours away. Is this the American dream? How had we fallen into this crazy lifestyle? We originally set out to just be simple people who loved Jesus, loved our neighbors, and loved our kids. What in the world happened?!

I called a friend whose kids were all grown and asked, "Did you ever feel like you were going crazy in this minivan world?"

He replied, "We complained about it all the time until they started to get their own licenses and drive themselves. Before we knew it they packed their bags and left for college. We sat here the other night saying we wished those minivan days were back. Though they were crazy, at least we were all together." His reply changed my perspective, and I began to appreciate this season of life.

Let me add some sanity to all the craziness. Our commitment as a family was to our basic values; this took precedence over all the activity. Our first commitment was time with Jesus and family devotions. We then prayed together to decide which activities to pursue with each new season. We wanted each of our four kids to have the opportunity to discover their interests and talents, and each area of involvement added complexity to our lives. These years caused the most difficulty staying focused on what we valued most.

Despite the struggle, we learned several responses that

helped us navigate the tension of supporting our kids' activities while staying true to our core family values.

OUR PROCESS: WE PRAYED ABOUT EVERYTHING

Philippians 4:6-7 says, "Be anxious for nothing, but in everything by prayer and supplication with thanksgiving let your requests be made known to God. And the peace of God, which surpasses all comprehension, will guard your hearts and your minds in Christ Jesus."

This Scripture became our key. Three times a year, we discussed our desires and planned events for the upcoming months. We talked with each kid in depth about their extra activities and asked them to take a week and pray about them with us. Then we came together in order for each person to share what he or she sensed from God.

We believed, with all of our hearts, if we prayed and looked after our kids' interests and to God's leadership, then we could trust Him with our plans. We allowed the peace of God among us to rule—sometimes leading us to do more and sometimes leading us to do less. If anyone expressed a lack of peace, we talked until we reached a place of agreement. At times, Laura and I were forced to make a tough decision before we had full agreement from the kids, but trust was maintained because we intentionally involved them in the process. Above all, we sought confidence that God was leading us, not our own desires.

OUR RULE: ONE THING AT A TIME

Until the kids reached fourth or fifth grade, we set a general rule allowing only one sport or extracurricular activity per child. This meant one in the fall, one in the spring, and one in the summer. Around the fourth grade many of the activities began to overlap so we decided to expand beyond our restrictions in order for our kids to try out new things to discover their gifts and passions.

Between fourth grade and ninth grade was our busiest time because of the frequent activities with no additional drivers beyond Mom or Dad. Involvement narrowed again in high school because they identified their gifts and talents and invested accordingly.

OUR INVOLVEMENT: AS MUCH AS POSSIBLE

From history and science fairs to community service projects to coaching sports teams, Laura and I stayed involved. As we have stated throughout the book, our top priorities were their personal character development and their spiritual lives. Our involvement allowed us to see them in many different settings and gave us a chance to challenge them when needed.

Our close involvement caused us to pull out of certain activities we felt contradicted our values or wrongly influenced our kids. We also regularly used activities to build relationships and share Jesus with other parents who didn't know the Lord. Sports fields are great mission fields for busy parents!

We do not regret being intimately involved, despite the added busyness.

OUR CAPACITY: MANAGING EXPECTATIONS OF OUR TIME

At times, I felt conflicting emotions while listening to a well-known athlete, scholar, or musician talk about the influence of their mom or dad. I would be inspired as they described how their parents never missed a ballgame or musical performance. Yet I felt defeated because we had four kids and only two of us. When everyone has an event at the same time, what do we do?

The kids knew we supported them, but I was still forced to balance my time between their events and a busy, sixty-hours-per-week job. I told them in advance when I saw a scheduling conflict, and they factored our availability into their involvement decisions.

Kids need our all-in support, but they also need a reality check of our availability. I found many parents make promises they cannot keep, which causes deep pain. Please be clear and honest with your kids so there is not regret later, either for them or for you, about missed opportunities.

We raised our kids to change the world. We should stay involved with them to give legitimate feedback, help, and growth along the way. World-changers don't live like everybody else. Once you decide on each child's activities, commit to them wholeheartedly. Evaluate after each season and pray through the next. Instead of viewing extracurricular activities as a hassle, treat them as a blessing. Activities are a way to learn and to grow, a way to develop as a young man or young woman, a way to learn how to organize, how to plan, and how to make decisions. Additionally, they are wonderful opportunities to minister to others. We look back, not with regret, but rather with great joy at our busiest years.

"I was very, very fearful as a child. Yes, I was afraid of the normal things like the dark and storms, but it was a fear that drove me to irrational thoughts and a lot of tears. I consistently ran to my parents' room at night, and they would pray for me and sometimes let me sleep between them. At a young age they had me memorizing lots of little Scriptures on overcoming fear, and they lovingly told me I couldn't sleep with them anymore but needed to lie in bed and talk to Jesus until I fell asleep. Step by step I overcame this deep fear. There is no way I could have overcome on my own. I would not have known where to start. Thankfully, my parents were there to coach me and walk me through it all."

LAUREN

CHAPTER 13

HELPING THEM TO OVERCOME

Do you not know that those who run in a race all run, but only one receives the prize? Run in such a way that you may win.
1 Corinthians 9:24

JIMMY

"Please don't leave me, Daddy. My tummy hurts."

These words marked Lauren's first few days of third grade. Every morning before school she woke up saying she had a stomachache and wanted to stay home. We took her to the doctor, who confirmed she was not sick. This was not a physical problem but an emotional one. We soon discovered she was fearful because she had a difficult time with spelling.

Every person has strengths and weaknesses. Learning to face our weaknesses, and ultimately overcoming them, is an essential part of building character. Parents need to help their children identify their weaknesses and then confront them together. This both addresses the present problem and also builds confidence for personal growth in the future.

You, the parent, have a powerful opportunity to shape the character of your child. You can empower them to believe they can overcome; you can challenge them to confront their weakness and their fear. This will position them for success in whatever they do, but it will require focus and time from you.

OVERCOMING ACADEMICALLY

Once we realized Lauren's problem, we worked with her every night to review her spelling words to prepare for her Friday tests. At times, we spent three hours side by side in the evening. By fourth grade, three hours turned to two hours; by sixth grade she caught up to her peers. She graduated with honors from high school and college and now has a degree in speech pathology. She chose this field to help others who struggle as she once did. As of this writing she is in graduate school, working on her Master's in Speech Pathology.

We made it through those days, not by avoiding the pain of her weakness but by teaching her how to overcome. Because we sat side by side, what could have been a place of deep failure and pain in her life became a place to build confidence. She discovered she could take on any challenge and succeed.

OVERCOMING SOCIALLY

Let's face it, kids can be awkward. While some find it easy navigating social settings, others find it extremely difficult. Either way, life requires us to interact with people, so we need to train our kids to do it well. Parents need to embrace the uncomfortable conversation of telling their child the areas in which they're socially awkward. Tell them the truth in love. If you don't, someone else will.

I remember a time when Caleb was being rejected at school. We knew about it because other parents and teachers told us there was a problem. Things were not going well socially for my older son. The thing was, he had absolutely no clue. Caleb was oblivious.

I had to get to the bottom of things. So, one day I visited his school at lunchtime, sitting down in the cafeteria along with him and his classmates as they ate. I simply wanted to watch how he interacted with his friends and what was causing his rejection. As I sat and observed, the problem became instantly clear.

Let me paint the picture.

I love my son. But the kid had an impressive set of buck-teeth at the time, with a space between his two front teeth, no less. In addition, the guy was a talker. After being bottled up all morning in class, lunch presented the perfect chance to let loose. He was so eager to speak he rarely waited to swallow his food. His surrounding peers were then subjected to a constant spray of half-chewed food and Caleb-spit. As I looked on, I understood the problem.

Something had to be done.

We were already navigating the "chew with your mouth closed" skill at home and thought we were progressing, but quickly realized no one was reminding Caleb at school. That day when he returned home I pulled him aside, described what I saw, and explained why the kids were rejecting him. Caleb still didn't think it was a big deal.

"Son," I said, making my tone clear, "this is socially unacceptable, and it's time to change."

"OK," he finally nodded.

The conversation was emotional and uncomfortable, but necessary. We overcame the problem together. And soon enough, he started eating and talking like a normal person.

At times, the most loving action a parent can do for their kid is to initiate a difficult conversation. We're tempted to avoid these talks because we know it will be emotional; we fear the pain of the moment so we simply say nothing. Unfortunately, passivity only leads to greater hurt. You avoid a painful moment but expose your child to the much deeper pain of rejection.

OVERCOMING PHYSICALLY

Abby competed in her first cross-country meet as a high school freshman. She'd practiced all summer to get ready for the competition, and I was so proud of her discipline and drive. We talked through the race beforehand, set a goal for her finish time, and decided we wanted her to finish in the top fifteen.

When that day finally arrived, I stood next to the starting line as she lined up with the other runners. The official raised his gun, pointed to the sky, and pulled the trigger. The blast had no sooner reached my ears when the runners were off, jockeying for a strong position on the track.

I could have stayed there cheering as my daughter faded into the distance. But let's just say I'm not that kind of dad. Instead I darted forward and ran alongside her outside the ropes for the first three hundred yards. After that, I sprinted across the field to the first mile marker to wait for her arrival. When she ran past I shouted as loud as I could, "You're right on pace at twentieth place!"

Abby reached the 2.5-mile marker in seventeenth place, and there were two girls within reach before finishing the 3.1-mile race. She was close to catching them, but I could see she needed help. Totally disregarding the opinions of others, I ran alongside her once again, shouting encouragement from outside the ropes. Entering the stadium, she caught one girl at the turn, with the other within striking distance. I stayed by her side until we were a hundred yards from the finish line and then I backed off, cheering her all the way through.

She passed the sixteenth runner with five yards to spare.

I ran up and hugged her like she had won the Olympics.

This might seem like an over-the-top bit of fathering. It was just a race, after all. But this was a victory for my daughter. And victories, even little ones, can be great teachers. What made this race so meaningful for Abby was that for most of her life she had never thought she'd be a runner.

LAURA

In junior high, we began working with Abby to develop healthy habits, including exercise, but she wasn't convinced it was necessary. Undaunted, we required her to either walk or run two miles daily five days a week. Let's just say she wasn't thrilled at the prospect. But we persevered, knowing if she developed a consistent rhythm of exercise she'd eventually learn to value it as a lifestyle.

In the years following that personal cross-country victory, she ran multiple half-marathons. She still runs long distances, is a certified personal trainer, and enjoys working out with her husband. Abby repeatedly expresses thankfulness for the way we trained her, even when she resisted.

OVERCOMING DISAPPOINTMENT

JIMMY

During the fall of Caleb's junior year in high school, he
excelled as a placekicker while also playing defensive back
on the varsity football team. Things were going well until one
Saturday afternoon. While playing soccer, he stepped on the
ball and sprained his ankle, or so he thought. He kept it taped
up for two weeks and even kicked successfully in the football
game, but he found it difficult to run and make cuts as a defensive back.

We eventually realized something was wrong. We visited an orthopedic doctor and learned Caleb had fractured his
ankle, effectively ending his football season and, even worse,
possibly compromising his basketball season.

He was forced to wait to start basketball until after Christmas because of his injury. Despite the setback, he attended
every practice to support and encourage his teammates. He
also worked hard physically to obtain the doctor's clearance.
Once cleared, he played a few junior varsity games and began
to travel with the varsity team, hoping to increase his playing
time or even start.

It never happened. Caleb did everything the coach asked,
but he would not let him play. As a dad, this was excruciating.
That year should have been his athletic peak. But instead, he
spent every game warming the bench, only playing a few minutes of a handful of blowout games.

I don't know if you've ever been there, but it's tough, let
me tell you. I alternated between anger toward the coach,
frustration with the situation, questioning my son's ability, and
even suspecting a hidden agenda. All the while, he continued
to sit game after game, showing outward support for the team
but dying on the inside.

Despite the pain, we chose to embrace disappointment as an opportunity for personal growth. Caleb came out a better person, more focused on God's plan for his life instead of athletics, more of a servant, and deeper in character all around. Laura and I grew as well. It's hard watching your child struggle, but we responded by praying more frequently, trusting God more deeply, and emphasizing character over outcomes.

Disappointment, though difficult, is a fundamental part of life. Everyone will face it. The difference between success and failure in the long run is how we respond to this disappointment. You can't shelter your child from disappointment, but you can coach them through it.

Thankfully, Caleb had a banner year as a senior in high school. Not only did he run back an interception for a hundred-yard touchdown, he finished basketball with a whole slew of awards both from the school and on a statewide level. I might be bragging on my son here, but so would you if you saw your boy overcome disappointment so well. Success—whether academic, social, or physical—comes at a cost. Prioritize setting aside time to coach and encourage your kid. You shape your child's response to failure and disappointment and instill courage in them to take on what seems impossible. Don't miss the chance to instill in them the confidence to overcome. You will never regret it.

"One of my favorite things about my parents' discipline process was that they never let us distance ourselves from them after discipline. Instead of letting me pull away, Mom and Dad pulled me in and let me know I was loved. They would hug me, tell me that they forgave me and Jesus forgave me, and put me right back into whatever the family was doing. I'm so thankful my parents made it clear that even though I needed to be corrected, that didn't mean I was pushed away from the family."

CALEB

CHAPTER 14

TRAINING THEM TO OBEY

Children, obey your parents in the Lord, for this is right. Honor your father and mother (which is the first commandment with a promise) so that it may be well with you, and that you may live long on the earth.

Ephesians 6:1-3

JIMMY

I looked across the yard and saw our four-year-old Abby by the fire pit. She picked up a can of lighter fluid, tipped it up high, and opened her mouth to take a big drink.

Horrified, I screamed across the yard, "Abby!" She immediately stopped and looked at me. "Put it down right now!"

As she dropped the can, she burst into tears and ran into my arms. I explained to her this was not a drink; this was poisonous and could hurt her. I held her close and thanked her repeatedly for stopping and immediately obeying Daddy. Training kids to immediately obey may not be popular, but it will save them from destruction—whether from childhood dangers or adolescent peer pressure.

Caleb learned the consequences of disobedience the hard way. A chain-link fence ran across our backyard, holding back the woods on the other side. As is common for most young boys, he was intrigued by the opportunity to explore. But he knew climbing on the fence was not allowed. We had already disciplined him once for doing it.

One day, while working in the kitchen, I heard a bloodcurdling scream from the backyard. I ran out the back door and saw Caleb at the bottom of the fence. I immediately realized what happened. He tried to climb over the fence to get to the woods; but when he reached the top, his foot slipped and he cut his face on the metal barbs. While he lay there wailing, blood dripping down his face, part of me wanted to scoop him up in my arms while another part wanted to shout, "I told you so!"

Eventually the doctor stitched him up, but to this day he still has a little scar on the left side of his face. His act of disobedience caused momentary pain but left a scar for life.

God asks us to obey Him because it's for our good. As parents, our desire was to see our children free from the bondage of sin, free to enjoy Jesus, and free to enjoy all God has for them. The way to realize this goal was for us to train, correct, and discipline our children in a loving and consistent manner. It may be painful for a moment, but it will save them from lasting damage.

OUR VISION FOR DISCIPLINE

LAURA

This book is all about discipleship. We are teaching our children the ways of God by taking them to the Word of God, modeling it ourselves, and training them in the right way. But this is a process, and it takes time—in fact, more time than you can even imagine. And if you have not already decided by now that this is part of your calling in life, this time-consuming process will more than frustrate you. It did not take long for us to figure out that our kids were not born obedient, so we had to come up with a process that would train and address the issues of their lives.

IT BEGINS WITH CLEAR EXPECTATIONS

We as parents have to be clear in what we are asking our children to do, as well as take the time to show them the right actions and responses they should have. We call this training. The Word tells us in Colossians 3:21, "Fathers, do not exasperate your children, so that they will not lose heart." We exasperate or frustrate them when they have no idea what they are to do. It is our job to show them and train them.

Let me say it this way.

When our kids were little, going to the store with three or four of them could be quite an experience (or can I say trial?). I call our large grocery store The Land of Temptation and Options. Let's face it, with so many amazing choices even I have to stay focused on buying what I need instead of what I want. So I had to come up with a plan. When we were about to go into the store, I would park the car and go through the routine. (Let me tell you, this happened over and over again).

"OK, guys. We are going to go into the store, and this is

what is going to happen. Abby and Lauren, you are going to walk by the cart. I want you to keep your hand on the cart unless I ask you to get something. You can be my helpers, but I want you to wait to be asked to help. Caleb, you are going to sit in the main basket and Daniel in the front. It is not OK to stand up. If either of you stand up in the basket, you will be disciplined when we get home. Also, we are going for the things on my list. Please do not ask for anything extra or reach for any candy. Does anyone have any questions, because now is the time to ask them?"

If there was a bit of distraction I would repeat the routine. And off we would go. Both the expectations and the consequences were clearly spelled out before we went in. If we went through the whole event with no surprises and full obedience, I would praise them in the car and tell them how proud I was of them for obeying me. Sometimes that obedience led to ice cream or a special treat. But if things didn't go as expected, without anger (maybe frustration, but not anger), we would go straight home and deal with the consequences. This was not convenient for me, but I knew that eventually it would stick and pay off later. When it comes to the full spectrum of disciplining our kids, we must make the expectations and consequences clear and be consistent in our follow-through.

OBEY CHEERFULLY, QUICKLY, AND COMPLETELY

JIMMY

We created a phrase we recited at our family devotions each morning in order to set expectations of obedience. We asked, "How do you obey?" and they replied in unison, "Cheerfully, quickly, and completely."

These three steps laid a foundation for their attitude, both in our home and before God. The Bible says if we love God, we will obey His commands (John 14:23). The Bible also says His commandments are not burdensome (1 John 5:3). By teaching kids the habit of obeying cheerfully, quickly, and completely, it created a lifestyle of joy in their relationship with God.

Cheerfully

Have you ever corrected a child only to see them respond with a mean face, stomping foot, or throwing a fit? In Philippians 2:14, Paul tells us to "do all things without grumbling" or complaining. This Scripture teaches that getting the job done with a good attitude is just as important as the task itself. Jesus talked over and over again about the attitude of the heart. Jesus criticized those who washed the outside of the cup but left the inside unclean (Matthew 23:25-26). Modeling our correction after these two Scriptures, we wanted the kids to obey from the heart with a happy attitude. We set an expectation every morning and lovingly enforced it.

If we asked a child to pick up their clothes, take out the trash, or come in from play, we expected them to do it with a great attitude. The appropriate response was "Yes, ma'am" or "Yes, sir" with a pleasant voice. When they did not respond rightly, we gave another opportunity by saying, "Let's try that again with the right attitude." If they again chose not to respond with the right attitude, we initiated the discipline process to reinforce cheerful obedience. Teaching your kids to obey cheerfully makes your home a peaceful place and trains your children to be a blessing to teachers, coaches, employers, and other authority figures for the rest of their lives.

LAURA

Whenever a guest visited our home, we expected our kids to look them in the eye and say hello. This seemed like an easy request, but for our two-year-old daughter Lauren, it felt like asking her to climb Mount Everest.

While waiting for a guest to arrive, we instructed Lauren on a proper greeting. "When someone greets you and says 'Hello, Lauren,' you respond by looking them in the eyes, smiling, and saying 'hello.'" Easier said than done.

She instead responded by hiding behind our legs or burying her face in our chest. My friend Melissa often came by the house during this time. Day after day, Melissa arrived and Lauren responded by hiding behind me. I asked Lauren to say hi. She did not obey. We went into the other room to go through the process of correction. We hugged. I explained the expectations again and we returned to try again. This often happened once, twice, three times. I sometimes wanted to give up and explain away her disobedience with excuses that she was tired or just not feeling well, but I knew this was something she had to overcome. She needed to push past her insecurity and look Melissa in the eye with a smile and say hello.

We eventually overcame. Today Lauren is warm, personable, and a great conversationalist. In college she had the job of giving tours at Baylor University, talking to parents and students on a daily basis. The hard work paid off, built up her confidence and set her up for life.

Quickly

JIMMY

Teaching your child to respond to your request the first time is important. We called this "first-time obedience." I've often seen kids ignore their parent's command to quit touching something at the store. When the child doesn't obey, the parent responds by initiating a countdown, saying, "I'm counting. You have until ten."

When they finally reach ten the kid is typically still disobeying. By this point, the parent is angry, either grabbing their child by the arm to force them or simply walking away and leaving their kid in a crying heap.

We chose to not live this way.

Before we explain more, we need to make something clear. If we want quick obedience, then we need to be careful and think before we ask. We are all guilty at times of just calling out things we want done flippantly and have no intention of really following up and making sure it was done. As we train our kids to respond quickly, we need to take the responsibility to think before we ask with the expectation and commitment that we will follow up if it is not done.

We didn't always do it right. This was something we had to learn. When our kids were young they loved to jump on the trampoline in the backyard. One day at dinnertime, I called out to them to come inside, and they responded by saying, "We hear you, Dad!"

A few minutes later, after they had not come in, I opened the door again and called out, "Come in now." Once again, they responded with, "Coming!" A few minutes later, because they still had not come inside, I opened the door and said, "Come in right now or you are going to be disciplined!" Finally, they came running in while I lectured them in frustration. I had been caught in the trap of not following through the first time. Everyone slips, and it was time to get back on track. Threats cause distance. Immediate correction brings relationship. The purpose of a threat is to avoid discipline through either nagging or a lecture. However, avoiding discipline doesn't deal with the sin.

One important lesson we have learned in our parenting is that when obedience is lacking in the kids, we have to look first at ourselves and make sure we are following through. Most likely our laziness has trained them to not respond and therefore increased the frustration in us. By enforcing first-time obedience, you avoid letting frustration build. And the more consistent you are in reinforcing that, the quicker their obedience will be.

When Laura and I caught ourselves stuck in this cycle of failing to follow through, we responded by apologizing to our kids for not being consistent to discipline them the first time. We took ownership for our lack of being clear and getting frustrated, and recommitted to our expectation of obeying cheerfully, quickly, and completely. When we went through this process, not only were our strained relationships restored, but also the children returned to obeying the first time. This requires hard work. But once it becomes habit, tension in the home goes down, relationship goes up, and parenting becomes joyful.

Completely

In addition to teaching our children to obey cheerfully and quickly, it's important for them to obey completely. Be clear with your expectation and decide what's important. There are many things our kids need to work on, but we can't give them a hundred different commands. This would exasperate them and you. Give simple and clear instruction and require their full compliance.

Cleaning their room was a great opportunity for our kids to learn this lesson. We began by explaining our full expectations. A clean room meant the bed is made, clothes are either hung in the closet or folded in the drawer, and toys are put away. Pretty straightforward and simple.

After breakfast, we asked our kids, "Did you clean your room?"

If they said yes we responded with, "That's great! I'm going to go up and check it out." If they fully obeyed their demeanor was peaceful. If they had not obeyed completely they responded by running ahead of us, saying, "Wait just a minute—I think I may have forgotten to do something."

They knew there would be consequences for partial obedience, not just nagging and threats. When your kids are convinced you will follow through with appropriate discipline, they will be diligent to fulfill your requests. This is training for life.

To teach obedience, start by choosing your area of focus and concentrate on it for a season. You cannot do everything at once, but you can start with something. Today our kids are grateful for the lessons learned early. By training them to respond well, regardless of their feelings, we trained them to be successful and to be a joy to others.

THE DISCIPLINE PROCESS

Before we got married, we resolved to make God and His Word central in our lives. We believed God's plans were the best for us. As a result, when we faced significant decisions, we responded by seeking God, His Word, and the counsel of godly people. This lifestyle of seeking God extended to how we disciplined our children. This Scripture stood out to us:

"We had earthly fathers to discipline us, and we respected them; shall we not much rather be subject to the Father of spirits, and live? For they disciplined us for a short time as seemed best to them, but He disciplines us for our good, so that we may share His holiness. All discipline for the moment seems not to be joyful, but sorrowful; yet to those who have been trained by it, afterwards it yields the peaceful fruit of righteousness" (Hebrews 12:9-11).

This passage gives a great framework for disciplining our children. First, it is normal and right to discipline our children. Second, it is for their good. The only motive is to help them and never to hurt them. Third, it is not always a joyful experience, but if done rightly and with love it will bring peace and righteousness in our home and in their hearts.

Several Proverbs support these basic truths:

"Poverty and shame will come to him who neglects discipline, but he who regards reproof will be honored" (13:18).

"Discipline your son while there is hope, and do not desire his death" (19:18).

"Listen to counsel and accept discipline, that you may be wise the rest of your days" (19:20).

"Foolishness is bound up in the heart of a child; the rod of discipline will remove it far from him" (22:15).

"For whom the LORD loves He reproves, even as a father corrects the son in whom he delights" (3:12).

LAURA

Let me start by addressing a sensitive issue. When we were first married, we immediately began to hang around other families that were following Jesus. Neither of us came from homes that did discipline in a way that really worked for us, so we wanted to learn from parents who were walking with God and whose kids exhibited the character and values we would want for our future children. We watched what those parents were doing and began to study the Word to back up what we saw, so we could make our own decision and be in agreement. Let me say that again: We wanted to be in agreement. What we watched others do and what we studied in the Word of God seemed to line up with the idea that using the rod of correction was to be taken at face value. We observed that finding a neutral object that was the focus of and part of the discipline process was essential in the process of disciplining. In seeking both the Word and counsel from godly parents, we used a small wooden spoon that can be applied to the fatty part of the bottom without bruising.

The goal is for the sting to curb unhealthy behavior, but in an environment of love. We chose a wooden spoon instead of our hand because we wanted our kids to view our hands as a place of comfort. We did not want them to fear us raising our hand. Additionally, we only spanked the fatty part of the bottom. We set a goal to never discipline out of anger. The goal of discipline was not to conveniently get our kids to get it together so we could get on with our agenda, but to train and shape their attitude and behavior.

JIMMY

While addressing this topic, we recognize there has been terrible abuse related to disciplining children. There is absolutely no excuse for that behavior. However, the sin of some people does not invalidate God's Word or the many examples of godly discipline shown by others. Like all things, anyone can wrongly use something meant for good. We committed to follow God's Word, even if it puts us at odds with pop culture. We have found that many people's hesitance to use the rod stems from fear and reaction to past pain. No decision based on our wounding or our fear will be healthy. When discipline is administered in a godly, loving, and caring environment, the kids are secure, peaceful, and self-controlled.

It is crucial that parents establish a clear process for disciplining their children. The discipline process gave us all a chance to keep our emotions in check. We found frustrations eventually boiled over in the absence of a clear process, regardless of discipline methods. By maintaining consistency we kept discipline focused on helping our children, not as an outlet for our frustration.

Even if your child is only two years old, he or she needs the process of loving discipline followed by affirmation in order to grow. Laura and I kept the steps very simple for our family. First, the offense occurred. We stopped the action and addressed the problem. "Caleb, you are not allowed to hit your sister; therefore, you will be disciplined."

We explained the offense and proceeded to tell him the number of spanks he would receive, normally three or four. We then leaned him over our legs and spanked his bottom. Immediately afterward, we hugged and held him. When he settled down, we discussed what just happened and why.

"Caleb, tell me again what you did."

"I hit my sister."

"Is that kind?"

"No"

"God wants us to be kind and protect our sister, not hit our sister. Now, what do you need to say?"

"Please forgive me."

We ended the process by looking him in the eyes and declaring that he is totally forgiven. We asked him to pray and ask Jesus for forgiveness because the offense isn't just against a person but ultimately against God. Following his prayer, we led him to make the appropriate restitution, in this case, with his sister, by telling her he is sorry for hitting her.

After the process is finished, we simply held him again and spoke words of kindness and restoration, such as, "We love you. You're our favorite six-year-old man in the world. You are a great man of God, and you are growing and learning. You are a kind man and one that defends and protects others. And I know that the Holy Spirit is going to help you learn this." We finally sent him on his way with no condemnation and no guilt.

We desired discipline to be clear and consistent so our children would not deal with ongoing guilt or anger. There is no condemnation after repentance. It would break my heart if, following the process, Caleb moped around the house saying, "I can't believe I did that." We would immediately reply, "Son, you are free. Don't worry about it. Now let's go play catch."

Discipline should lead to a restored relationship, not perfection or shame. This is how God leads us; we in turn model His love to our kids. Prompt and loving discipline sets your child free to enjoy grace and relationship.

DIFFERENT FORMS OF DISCIPLINE

People often promote other forms of discipline such as time out, grounding, or removing privileges. Though at times these forms might be appropriate and you may choose to use these, we chose spanking as our consistent method. We believe spanking best reflects grace because it confronts the issue of sin and disobedience but then quickly moves to a place of immediate restoration, eliminating the ongoing condemnation that is unresolved. Immediate consequences gave us the freedom to have both structure and continual connection with our kids.

We did not ground our young kids because we did not

want them to deal with condemnation. Many times if a parent confronts a problem by sending their kids away to their room or grounding them, it produces a sense of condemnation. The message is "I sinned. Therefore, I will now pay for it by being isolated from my family relationships."

Kids need consequences; but our discipline should align with God's Word, both in method and in heart. Biblically, the purpose of discipline is to inflict temporary pain to train children to later reap the blessing of righteousness, all done in an environment of love and a lot of training. Healthy discipline empowers our children to later grasp the power of grace—both the pain of sin and the joy of forgiveness.

LAURA

This is the method that we chose. Whatever the method you choose, we recommend discipline that leads to immediate restoration. By the time our kids were eleven or twelve years old, we found that we rarely had to discipline them this way. At this point we were having healthy conversations about right and wrong choices, appropriate responses, repentance, and personal responsibility. One amazing thing we found is that as the kids got older they actually invited us into the process of helping them make good decisions and changing. If we came to an issue that needed discipline, our kids would willingly help us talk through what was the best form of correction that would help them remember and change. Now as adults, our kids recall the times of discipline and restoration to be some of the sweetest memories of their lives. They knew we loved them and wanted the best for them. Our discipline process left them feeling restored, loved, and a part of the family.

DEALING WITH EXCUSES

JIMMY

When our children were young, they demonstrated incredible creativity to avoid discipline. "I forgot! I forgot!" was a common plea in our home. We responded by saying, "I am so sorry you forgot, but this spanking will help you remember not to forget." Again, if expectations are not clear and consequences are not consistent, children will feel insecure.

We enforced discipline when our kids forgot, when they were tired, and when they had a hard day. Why? Because sin is always destructive. We wanted to teach our children to respond rightly despite how they felt. Isn't that real life? Don't we as adults have to pull it together and do many things we don't feel like doing? Validating excuses sets a harmful precedent. One of the common sayings in our home was, "If you learn to obey Mom and Dad, you will learn to obey Jesus." God has great plans and promises for our children, but they will miss them if they don't respond to His voice.

RIGHT LANGUAGE CREATES RIGHT ATTITUDE

Children are a blessing, especially to adults, when they show honor and respect. We taught our kids to respond to us and other adults by saying "yes, sir" and "yes, ma'am." We also required them to address other adults using their titles, Mr. and Mrs. Some believe this practice is either old fashioned or limited to southern culture. We believe it created a consistent reminder for them to respect authority and adults.

Recently, my two boys ordered food at the airport food court by addressing the lady behind the counter with "yes, ma'am" and "no, ma'am." She was overwhelmed by their respect and commented their reply gave her hope again for the next generation. This simple gesture opened a door for us to share the love of Jesus. Many times we have been shown great favor because of our kids showing respect and honor. Instead of simply putting up with our kids, adults want them around.

TRAINING THE OLDER WILL TRAIN THE YOUNGER

LAURA

I often overheard Abby or Lauren instructing Caleb or Daniel to obey, though the boys didn't always appreciate their big sisters trying to enforce our rules. But we knew Abby and Lauren were merely trying to save their brothers from unneeded spankings. Caleb at times instructed Daniel on what was right and wrong. Daniel, poor guy, had no one to lead. When the boundaries are clear, everybody helps one another.

DANIEL'S STORY

Because we limited media time, we set a rule in our home requiring our kids to ask permission to turn on the TV. One day I walked into the house and heard the TV blaring. I looked across the room and saw two little legs sticking out below the almost-closed doors of the entertainment center. Daniel was standing behind the doors, fully believing he was hiding and no one could see him.

I laughed for a bit, but I also knew he was being disobedient and I needed to address the situation. I walked over and said, "Daniel, what are you doing?"

He looked at me with shocked little eyes and replied, "Nothing."

"No, Daniel. You aren't doing 'nothing,' you are disobeying. You are watching the TV without asking for permission."

With downcast eyes he asked, "Am I going to get a spanking?"

"Yes, buddy, because you disobeyed you will be corrected."

I followed through with the correction process, and as I was holding him at the end, I decided to use this as a teaching moment. "Did you know there is someone in this world you can't hide from? He sees everything you do. Do you know who that person is?"

"Yes, Mommy," he said.

"Who is it, buddy?" I asked.

"It's Caleb. He sees everything."

I held him close, laughing hysterically.

"No, buddy. Caleb may be good at seeing a lot of things, but God is the One who sees everything you do. He even knows the number of hairs on your head. He loves you and only has good plans for you. Anything He sets as a boundary is for your good."

By training our children in love, respect, and honor, we shaped them for the rest of their days. Unlike what you normally hear, our best times with our kids have been their teenage and young adult years. The foundation of discipline and consistency we laid early on has borne great fruit and delight.

JIMMY

Many parents are afraid to discipline their kids. If the parents grew up in a legalistic home, they may fear being overbearing. If they grew up in a passive home, they may push too hard. The keys to balance are always love and relationship.

Ultimately, following God's Word in an environment of grace and love always works. Work through your own pain and fears so you can focus on what is best for your child. Commit to discipline them in love so you too can train them for life.

"Purity. I think every parent hopes their child will reach their wedding day as a virgin. Only by the grace of God and my parents' guidance was I able to give that to my husband. By no means am I perfect, but to me, purity is entirely a matter of the heart. My parents protected me and set me up for godliness, then Jesus marked me and held me there. The five reasons I believe helped me to stay pure are: the ring from my father I wore from my thirteenth birthday until my wedding day reminding me I was not my own, my father's constant affirmation and intentionality, my parents' fervent prayers, my parents' personal choices and implementation of media in our home, and being taught to individually spend daily time in the presence of God."

CHAPTER 15

PROTECTING PURITY

Blessed are the pure in heart, for they shall see God.
Matthew 5:8

JIMMY

When the Soviet Union finally collapsed in 1991, it opened a door into a vast land that had been cut off from the world for decades. All across the Eastern bloc, people experienced a bombardment of new ideas—everything from Christianity to Hollywood.

As part of this new mission field, we had the opportunity to start a church in the country of Mongolia. One night while visiting a family there, I had a unique experience. Reclining into their tattered couch, I told different stories from the Bible and explained the power of God to heal and forgive. As I shared, I noticed an American movie playing on the television in the background. When the film led into a sexual scene, I turned away. But I was horrified to watch this family's young daughter walk over to the TV and start touching the screen, as if mesmerized by the images.

"No!" I compassionately yelled, scooping her up in my arms and turning off the TV. I was moved to tears thinking of this precious little girl's innocence being robbed in a moment. Not only was the family in shock, but I was taken aback at my intense response. I couldn't help but think of my own little girls and my heart to protect them as I held this little girl in my arms and began to talk to the parents about this situation. I explained to them that God loves us and created us for innocence and purity. I shared how allowing children to watch inappropriate sexuality will affect their perception of love and relationships. They tried their best to understand, but I realized that such a new way of thinking would take a while for them to comprehend.

We serve as the gatekeepers of our home. The word gatekeeper means "guardian or monitor, the one who controls the access to something." We, as the parents, are responsible for what comes into our home. It is our responsibility to protect our children from the onslaught of the media and its agenda to rob our kids of their purity and innocence. Times have changed. When I was a kid, if I wanted to see sex or pornography, I had to stay up late and hunt down the stations that were showing it. Sure, there were prime time shows that were subtly giving me the message that sex outside of marriage was okay and the norm, and that shaped a lot of my mindset as a young teenager, putting me on the wrong path. But nowadays, sex and lust come at you all day long. Sexuality pops up on the screen of a smart phone even when we're not looking for anything. It's aggressive, and it has an agenda.

1 Peter 5:8 tells us to "be of sober spirit, be on the alert. Your adversary, the devil, prowls around like a roaring lion, seeking someone to devour." Parents, we have to be on the alert, stay engaged in this media agenda, and be proactive with our kids on what they are exposed to and what they have access to. It is our job to create a safe environment in our home where their purity is protected. This protection empowers our kids to later give to others and not walk with a relational limp themselves.

A pure heart sets us free from the lies of guilt and shame. Sexuality is everywhere in our culture; not surprisingly, so is sexual sin and brokenness. The gift of purity is powerful, empowering your kids to experience a healthy marriage, live in personal wholeness, and ultimately to help set others free. Purity is countercultural and is difficult, but you will never regret fighting for it. As stated in Scripture, "Blessed are the pure in heart, for they shall see God" (Matthew 5:8). So let's break it down to those venues that fight for our kids' purity.

MUSIC

LAURA

Music is powerful. Though I haven't intentionally listened to secular music for over three decades, I still find myself easily singing every word to certain songs from my childhood when I hear them playing in a store. The words of songs I have not heard in thirty years are imbedded in my mind and stir up old memories and emotions.

Jimmy and I began to seriously pursue God in college, and I knew I needed rewiring. I grew up listening to Phil Collins, Bread, the Carpenters, REO Speedwagon, and Kenny Rogers—amazing artists with the incredible skill of stirring my emotions. When I asked God what would be one step to change, I felt the Holy Spirit offer the challenge to cut off all secular music and let my heart be cleansed and renewed by washing it with worship. I found that this step created an environment of peace in my heart, and my mind was more set on God than my feelings and desires. Since then I have developed the habit of making that our main musical diet, so that naturally flowed into our home when we were married and later had kids.

JIMMY

We established the habit of playing Christian music in our home before we had kids, believing it would set a foundation for our family. We knew our kids' music preferences would be shaped in their early years. Our goal was far bigger than merely avoiding the world; we wanted our children to experience the power of true worship, fully believing they would never be satisfied by anything less.

We saturated our home with worship, nearly twenty-four hours a day, seven days a week. We embraced every opportunity to host small group meetings at our house in order for our kids to see God's people worshipping outside of the church building. Ultimately, during their developmental years, we sought to expose our kids to true worship while also protecting them from worldly influences as much as possible.

Many people questioned our approach, wondering why we took such a strong stance with music and avoided what some perceived as innocent, fun songs. We knew our kids had the rest of their lives to listen to whatever they chose, so we opted to maximize their early years as a chance to build their desire for God.

LAURA

Some believers accused us of being too legalistic, but we had a completely different perspective. We loved clean, fun songs and worship; our family had a blast with music! Our perspective was that God is the creator of fun and joy and His presence is better than anything the world offers.

Our experience mirrored the Psalms: "For a day in Your courts is better than a thousand outside" (Psalm 84:10). But embracing this path required us to walk a narrow road. To this day our kids don't feel deprived at all by not having listened to secular music. As they have become adults and made their own decisions, they have branched out here and there enjoying a clean secular song, but they always say worship music is their favorite music. In fact, they have expressed deep thankfulness for us creating an appetite for God's presence.

TV AND MOVIES

"The eye is the lamp of the body; so then if your eye is clear, your whole body will be full of light" (Matthew 6:22).

"Watch over your heart with all diligence, for from it flow the springs of life" (Proverbs 4:23).

Kids' habits are formed at a very early age, and we wanted our children to develop the habit of turning away from evil and turning toward purity. To that end we both limited and monitored their media input.

We set a rule allowing no more than thirty minutes of television or video per day (besides their quiet time video). There were exceptions when we watched movies together or they watched something with friends, but we felt it important to establish a guideline. We also chose not to have cable TV during their young years because we did not want it to be the centerpiece of our home or have any of us tempted to view something inappropriate.

JIMMY

In their early years we let our kids watch selected videos or PBS kids' shows we had already prescreened. Laura and I took it further by committing to not watch anything ourselves we didn't want our kids to watch. Our family carefully selected movies, using reviews on Web sites like "Screen It!" or "Plugged In." We particularly avoided sexual content, extreme violence, and the use of God's name in vain. A friend later introduced us to the ClearPlay device, which filters profanity, sensuality, and other areas of concern according to your content preferences, allowing us to broaden our options.

Additionally, we only watched movies and documentaries that supported our values. When our kids grew older we allowed them to choose educational or historical movies that promoted different values in order to facilitate discussions about differing worldviews. We followed up with questions, such as "What was good about this show? What was not good? What did you learn?"

These standards sometimes excluded our kids from birthday parties and gatherings with school friends. Despite those disappointments, we believed protecting them was worth not compromising. If they were not allowed to attend a party, we replaced it with something fun so they wouldn't feel they were missing out. We invited a friend to sleep over, watched a movie as a family, or hosted a spontaneous family game night.

This is important. Our kids remember the fun we had together far more than the experiences they missed. You can't set rules without relationship. We really wanted our kids to have fun, even though rules were necessary to protect them. Our kids are grateful for the high standards we set because these boundaries kept their hearts pure.

A YOUNG MAN'S STORY

A young college student came to me because he was troubled by a movie his friends asked him to watch. He declined to go because he heard the movie contained a nude scene. He had recently finished a long journey of finding freedom from pornography and sexual relationships and knew if he saw this movie it would reignite past sin struggles. Though he felt confident in his decision not to attend, he was disturbed when his friends accused him of legalism. He sat in my office and asked, "Am I legalistic? What is the balance? How do we deal with media when it comes to sexual things?"

I sought to bring a clear perspective to his confusion by replying, "You have a seventeen-year-old sister. What if I or somebody else began to tell you they were drawn to her sexually? How would you respond? Hopefully with righteous anger!"

"Let's take another scenario. What if someone asked you to look in the window of a couple having an intimate relationship? You'd be shocked! You could be arrested if you agreed."

By now I had his full attention.

Finally, I began to put the pieces together. "Every time you watch a movie with explicit sex scenes, or view soft pornography or hard pornography, you need to realize you are watching real people. Those women are someone's wife or sister or mother. If you detach yourself from the reality of relationship you will miss the heart of God." Our conversation was intense, but he got the point. This man found freedom and continues to live free today. Bringing it down to real relationships and real people gave my friend context for making healthy choices in what he viewed.

Laura and I also trained our kids with this perspective; if Jesus wouldn't enjoy watching it then why would we watch it? Our ultimate goal is relationship with Jesus—more than anything else. If any media in our life hinders our friendship with Him then it simply isn't worth it, no matter what anyone else says.

A YOUNG WOMAN'S STORY

Laura and I once counseled a college student struggling with bulimia. Eating disorders are often related to parental relationships, so I asked about her relationship with her father. She answered, "My dad was a leader in the church, and our family was really close. But something happened when I was in the eighth grade, while I was developing as a young lady. We went to see the movie Titanic as a family, and I sat next to my dad. A scene came on with a topless woman, and I immediately turned to look at my dad. I saw him with a funny look on his face and noticed he was taking it all in. I looked down at my own chest and thought, 'Does he look at me that way? I never want him to look at me like this.'"

"I began to pull away from him. I wondered how he was looking at me every time I walked by him. I soon decided I wanted to look different and began to wear baggy clothes. I hoped my body would shrink so my daddy would not look at me that way."

These are hard stories to hear, and may sound extreme, but they are true. Laura and I both began to cry as our hearts broke for her. I realized once again how powerfully media affects our kids. It determines how they see themselves and how they see the world around them. It matters.

VIDEO GAMES

We had two primary concerns with video games: We wanted to curb the influence of sensuality and violence driving many games, and we knew video games are addictive by nature. Studies show kids under the age of five should not regularly play video games because it creates an adrenaline addiction and they will go back to it repeatedly as a place of comfort.

Reporter Nick Bilton recalled saying to Steve Jobs, "So, your kids must love the iPad?" Jobs responded, "They haven't used it. We limit how much technology our kids use at home." Chris Anderson, father of five and former editor of Wired, told Bilton that he and his wife also limit their kids' use of technology. When asked why, he said, "That's because we have seen the dangers of technology firsthand. I've seen it in myself, I don't want to see that happen to my kids" ("Steve Jobs was a Low-Tech Parent," *New York Times*, September 10, 2014).

Of course, there is a balance. Technology is not innately evil, nor are video games. Just use discernment. Games that contain violence or sexuality are clearly off limits for obvious reasons. But if certain apps on phones, iPads, or other devices are clean and constructive or even educational, just make sure and set clear time boundaries. This way, your kids will develop the discipline of moderation that they will carry into their later years.

INTERNET

The most important step we took to preserve our kids' purity was not allowing computers in their room with Internet access. Everything on the computer was done in a public area. In their younger years, our kids were required to ask permission in order to access the Internet. This provided an environment of accountability for all of us and encouraged us to live with integrity.

We need to remember that the Internet is powerful. A computer can be used for productive reasons, but when handled wrongly it becomes dangerous, and even deadly. Don't put that power in your kids' hands if you're not willing to monitor its use.

In our day and age, we must go to greater lengths than our parents in order to protect our children's innocence. Evil and sin are never more than a click away. Please don't give full access to a powerful device like a smart phone or tablet computer with Internet to your teenager without some kind of filter. Powerful things need strong boundaries. I know grown men who disable the Internet on their cell phones because they know the temptation of sin on the Internet is too great. These are godly men, men who spend time with Jesus every day, are happily married and committed to their spouses, and stay involved with their churches. If a godly man disables Internet access on his phone because he knows he may not be able to handle it, don't assume a sixteen-year-old kid is mature enough to resist temptation.

Social networking is another place of temptation. If your child is a part of a social network (Facebook, Instagram, Twitter, etc.), then you should be a part of that social network as well. If your kid's Facebook profile is open to their friends, then you need to be one of their Facebook friends so you can see what's going on.

LAURA

This is a first step, but you need to realize you cannot simply be a Facebook friend and expect to know what's happening. We have to check. Many parents fall into the mindset of believing the best of their kids and trusting that their kid is not using their device in a destructive way. We cannot give boundaries and simply assume they'll be respected. Your child may not be doing anything wrong at all, but it's always worth checking in order to protect them. In fact, if your kid knows you are looking at their conversations, they will be more likely to stay away from a danger trail. Sin is rampant in our culture, and terrible things can happen, even with the "best kids" from the "best families."

I also want to address an issue of texting; not only personal texting but group texting. In one way it has revolutionized time and made it easy to communicate to a large number of people. On the other hand, a trend with young kids is to dump their feelings and opinions on these groups and create a wave of gossip, bullying, and rejection. If our kids have the power to use these things, let's empower them to use them for good and not for the destruction of others.

Words are hard to take back, and we have no idea the ripple effect one word can have on someone else. If your kids are using group communication with their phones, let them know that you are going to be checking it and making sure the communication is edifying and unifying.

JIMMY

Ultimately, everyone needs accountability; it can never be underestimated. I'm fifty years old, and someone knows where I am twenty-four hours a day. I have been faithful to my wife and faithful to the standards we communicated in this book.

At the same time, I don't trust myself as far as I can throw a stick. If I need to be accountable with the Internet, TV, movies, and alone time, how much more does a seven- or seventeen-year-old kid! Accountability is healthy; it recognizes the importance of a life of purity and integrity, and it understands the depth of worldly temptations. Let your kids know that you are in this together with them.

LAURA

There is no way for us to change the world if we are of the world. Parents have the opportunity to create an environment of holiness, purity, joy, and laughter. We have the opportunity to whet our children's appetites for the things of God. We cannot control everything that comes at them, but we can prepare them at a young age to be on the offensive in this world. I am absolutely convinced that if you are reading this book, you have the belief that your child was created for things far better than destruction and even normalcy. We can raise kids who are free, kids who will change the world. Purity will require you to live differently, but you will never regret it. Not for a moment.

"I remember a quote my parents use to say: 'If you don't work, you don't eat.' Not words of condemnation for us, but more of an expectation that we all had a part to play because life takes hard work. From daily chores in the house to being diligent with our schoolwork, or from babysitting to starting our own businesses, our parents taught us the value of being responsible. In order to succeed in life, they taught us that working diligently was always a major part of the formula."

LAUREN

CHAPTER 16

TEACHING A WORK ETHIC

The plans of the diligent lead surely to advantage,
but everyone who is hasty comes surely to poverty.
Proverbs 21:5

CALEB

I first competed in a track meet in the seventh grade. In my mind track had always been equated with a group of highly motivated and athletic students who were committed to working hard enough to win. Reality quickly set in when I soon realized that most of my classmates had never even seen a track.

In fact, it seemed like their primary motivation was as simple as a free T-shirt and a day off of school!

I quickly embraced the laid-back attitude and looked forward to my free day out in the sun. Unfortunately, Dad had different ideas. He challenged my approach, telling me that if I was going to compete, I should give my best effort. We soon created a plan for me to run 400-meter sprints every day after school. We mapped out the distance together around our church parking lot. With more than a little prodding from Dad, I ran each day, convinced I was the only kid in the whole city running sprints outside in the Texas heat.

In hindsight, I learned a few important principles: First, success requires a lot more work and discipline than you think it will. Second, excellence should always be the standard in everything we do. Third, short legs weren't made to run 400-meter sprints.

JIMMY

Laura and I committed to teach our children the value of diligence and hard work in every aspect of life—school, exercise, chores, and their first job, to name a few. Work is a part of life. Unfortunately, most people were not taught to view it correctly. People often consider work to be a burden, but we believe it becomes a joy when done in partnership with God.

We were given eighteen years to train our children and believed if we taught them to be diligent in their responsibilities then we would not have to be concerned about their ability to lead a family or the opportunity to be successful in their vocation. However, to instill diligence in our children, we had to be diligent to coach, train, and teach.

DILIGENCE IN THE HOME

We created a chore chart outlining expectations for each kid. It started out with simple responsibilities such as brushing your teeth, making your bed, picking up your clothes, and having your quiet time. When the kids were young, these basic chores helped them develop good habits.

As they grew older, we added individual chores to help us run the household, including taking out the trash and doing the laundry. We added a "special category" for anything extra we needed to get done.

The Seiberts were a team, and we needed the team to keep things running. To support this mindset, we developed a game called "clean sweep." When Laura or I called it out, everyone picked up all their items throughout the house. Keeping the house clean and functioning was a group effort.

Chores weren't an option, and we expected them to be done with joy. These responsibilities helped us (the parents) manage the home, but more importantly developed a work ethic in our children.

We're often asked whether or not we gave our children an allowance for completing their chores. We gave them ten cents for every chore successfully completed (payment increased with age). Our kids checked a box on their chart for each chore they finished, around five to seven things a day.

If we had to nag them to do a chore, no allowance! In these situations, they were still required to do the work, they just weren't paid for it. At the end of the week, we added up all the checked boxes and distributed their allowances accordingly. This philosophy taught them to do their work with joy and offered accountability for their responsibilities. It didn't always work smoothly; some weeks we forgot to pay the allowance or we nagged them more than we should have. Despite the setbacks, our plan gave us a process to teach and train our kids to be diligent.

Our friends Vincent and Tonja Carpenter were more thorough and consistent with their kids' chores than we were, so we thought you should hear from them.

How the Carpenters Did Chores

VINCENT

My wife, Tonja, and I started our parenting journey with the belief that our children were a blessing to us from God and they were called to be a blessing to others. This influenced our approach to teaching our children about chores. We viewed chores as an opportunity to teach our kids to be great family members, college roommates, future spouses, and employees.

We began teaching our kids chores soon after they learned to walk. As infants, our children's first chore was to take their own diapers to the garbage can. When our children were around eighteen months of age they enjoyed watching Tonja fold clothes. So, she taught them to fold face towels.

During each of our kids' toddler through early elementary years, we continued to add responsibilities such as making their bed, washing dishes, and cleaning the bathroom. By age eight or nine, each of our five children could essentially do every chore in the house except cook a meal. Tonja introduced food preparation around age ten or when they grew tall enough to reach the back of the oven safely. At these earlier ages the children found chores fun, which made it easier to instill chores as a healthy lifestyle.

One of the best fruits of introducing chores early is that it motivated all of our children to work. With five kids living off a single income, expenses like multiple summer camps or mission trip fees can be a challenge. When our first two sons wanted to attend summer camp, they felt led to work odd jobs to pay the cost. One of our kids took a trip to Africa with the youth group and raised the entire amount himself.

We created a family culture of hard work by casting vision for each member to be a contributor.

Diligence in School Work

JIMMY

School provided a great way to build a work ethic in our children. From the beginning of their education, we focused more on their diligence and interaction with others than we focused on the grades they received.

We believed that if our kids worked hard, demonstrated responsibility, and honored what was asked of them, their grades would take care of themselves.

What if your kid struggles with school? Two of our kids did find school to be difficult. We responded by continuing to focus on character while also providing them additional support. We sat by their side for hours as they learned to master spelling, writing, or math. We hired a tutor when their learning needs were beyond our ability. We helped our children discover their unique learning style so that they could be successful even in the areas in which they struggled.

Whatever the learning problems, avoid passivity at all costs. Stay engaged in order to position your child to thrive in the learning process. If learning is a weak area in your kid's life, then this is your opportunity to teach them to overcome and work through difficulty. Men and women with a strong work ethic and godly character will impact society in a powerful way, even if they never become a rocket scientist or cure cancer.

Vision for Education

LAURA

"Why do I have to learn this? Why is this relevant? When will I ever use this again?" were common complaints from our kids, and many days we silently agreed with them (especially when it came to geometry or calculus). These questions exposed a waning sense of purpose.

Our kids needed vision for education.

As a solution we helped them see they were not simply learning abstract math formulas, but also learning to work with people, learning to think critically, and learning to press through difficulty. Schooling is far more than imparting knowledge. It is a powerful opportunity to build character that will serve as the foundation for their life and ultimately their ability to serve others.

As they got into high school and we began to discuss their futures, we recognized it was a big decision with significant ramifications and required even more vision. We felt led to help them approach the decision of future education with a missional philosophy: What will empower you to serve others yet still provide for your needs? What are you passionate about? Who do you want to help? Where do you want to see change in the world?

Abby had wanted to be a nurse since she was four years old. She grew up reading biographies of Florence Nightingale and Clara Barton. I have a picture of her as a young child wearing a homemade nursing outfit, complete with an old fashioned nursing hat. Her passion hit a roadblock in high school when she began to find math and science increasingly difficult. She struggled to grasp the concepts and spent hours studying to make A's.

Despite her best efforts, she realized the limit of her abilities and, in response, pursued a social work degree in college because it required less math and science. She received good grades and enjoyed what she was learning, but felt unsettled internally. She eventually reached a breaking point the day before the spring semester of her sophomore year. That morning she called me and through tears blurted out, "Mom, I can't do it anymore. I know I am fighting my calling. I'm trying so hard to embrace social work, but I know I am supposed to be a nurse. I have to switch my major, but I am so scared."

I called Jimmy, we prayed together, and we were in full agreement with Abby. It was time to change. I immediately drove to meet her at the school, and together we spent the day talking with different departments in order to rearrange her schedule. She needed to take a microbiology course and a statistics class for her new degree, and they both started the next day. We walked to the bookstore to search for her new textbooks and both felt intimidated when she pulled out a massive biology textbook.

I'll never forget that moment. Confronted with the reality of her own weakness, she stood in sudden turmoil. After several tense seconds, Abby finally exhaled a deep breath and pointed to the book, declaring, "In the name of Jesus, I will conquer you."

This story still makes me tear up. I am so proud of her. Four years later Abby graduated summa cum laude with her BSN. At this writing, she's working in a military hospital in Okinawa, Japan.

Diligence is not easy, but it's worth it. By learning to work hard and conquer both our fear and weakness, we are empowered to follow our calling. Embrace a larger vision of education than just making grades. Inspire your kids to maximize their years in school in order to build a strong foundation of character. God has a powerful plan for their life. Use this time to prepare them for it.

TEACHING THEM HOW TO WORK HARD

In addition to school, chores, and athletics, we taught our kids the value of a work ethic through working an actual job. Mission trips provided an initial motivation to train them. We asked them each to pray about an amount to contribute to their portion of the trip. Then we helped them find odd jobs such as babysitting, mowing lawns, or raking leaves. These jobs taught them how to be excellent in what they did, how to communicate with adults, and how to manage money.

Starting a business proved to be a great training opportunity for several of our kids. Caleb began mowing lawns when he was twelve with eight-year-old Daniel as his helper. He started with two lawns and expanded to eight over the next four years. When he was sixteen, they and a friend started a lawn business that eventually grew to over one hundred lots. The boys learned how to run heavy equipment, pull a trailer, interact with customers, lead work crews, and manage financial books. But more importantly, they learned how to work hard.

Our daughter Lauren started a business with a friend teaching swimming lessons. While in high school, the girls spent several nights attending Red Cross training in order to become certified swim instructors. Their business grew to train over one hundred kids in the summer.

While these businesses sound great, they came at a cost. Jimmy spent countless days hauling equipment and solving problems. I spent hours on a weekly basis lifeguarding at the pool and escorting little kids to the bathroom. Every family is given unique opportunities and faces unique challenges. Take advantage of these in order to train your kids.

TRAINING KIDS TO WORK IN AN AGE OF ENTITLEMENT

JIMMY

People regularly complain about a growing culture of entitlement. Many kids are given everything they want from an early age, to the point that they feel entitled to their wants without the need to work for them. We chose a different approach.

We provided for our kids' needs but required them to work for the additional things they desired. This taught them the value of a dollar. Our family seldom had abundant financial resources, but we did provide abundant opportunities to grow and to learn. Each kid left our house with a work ethic, which is a far greater gift than material possessions. We sought to raise our kids according to Proverbs 12:24, "The hand of the diligent will rule, but the slack hand will be put to forced labor"; not in accordance with the materialistic culture surrounding us.

I do not regret teaching our children to work diligently. This gift is more valuable than a large inheritance and ultimately prepared them for the future. Don't miss this opportunity.

"We grew up with three zip lock baggies in our sock drawers. One for tithe, one for missions, and one for savings. The rest of the money we earned we had in our wallets for spending. It's how we were taught to prioritize our money. One of the greatest things I am grateful for is learning the joy of giving. We had so much fun being able to pull out our missions money or even dip into our savings to give to a unique need in somebody's personal life or something going on in the world. Giving is an addicting feeling, one that has carried into my adult life. Thank you Mom and Dad!"

CHAPTER

17

MONEY AND POSSESSIONS

But store up for yourselves treasures in heaven,
where neither moth nor rust destroys, and where thieves
do not break in or steal; for where your treasure is, there your
heart will be also.
Matthew 6:20-21

JIMMY

"Dad, are we rich or are we poor?" twelve-year-old Caleb asked. I thought for a moment before replying, "I don't know, buddy. What do you think?"

"Well, I know some rich people, and we aren't rich. But I know some poor people, and we aren't poor." He paused for a moment before finishing his thought. "You know, Dad, I think we're just right."

No one is born content. Laura and I spent many long years learning contentment because rewiring an adult's mindset is especially difficult. We determined to spare our children this pain by imparting a healthy perspective on money and possessions at an early age.

As we've shared repeatedly, we chose to live by a biblical worldview rather than a cultural worldview. This is perhaps the most important aspect of parenting without regret. This is especially true regarding the contrast between our culture's materialistic perspective and the Bible's view of money.

The apostle Paul's words in Philippians set the standard for us: "Not that I speak from want, for I have learned to be content in whatever circumstances I am. I know how to get along with humble means, and I also know how to live in prosperity; in any and every circumstance I have learned the secret of being filled and going hungry, both of having abundance and suffering need. And My God will supply all your needs according to His riches in glory in Christ Jesus" (4:11-12,19).

This Scripture, along with several others, transformed our perspective on money and possessions. We summarized our understanding with three phrases: Live simply. Work diligently. Give generously. Since we discussed working diligently in the last chapter, let's focus on simplicity and generosity.

LIVE SIMPLY

Laura and I enjoy material possessions as much as anyone. We appreciate nice things and all that God has given us, but we did not want that to be the focus of our lives.

When we started college, we followed the same life path as everyone else we knew: Get through college, earn a degree, make a lot of money, and build wealth for the future. But when God miraculously captured our hearts, the purpose of life grew to something far beyond what this world has to offer.

LAURA

I remember reading Matthew 6:24: "No one can serve two masters; for either he will hate the one and love the other, or he will be devoted to one and despise the other. You cannot serve God and wealth." This Scripture challenged me to make sure money was not the driving motivation in my life. My real purpose is to love Jesus and love others, not to live comfortably.

Like many newly married couples, we did not start our life together with a lot of money, but God challenged us to go further. Rather than immediately building wealth, we started a new ministry, without a salary, and moved to the inner city. Though money was not abundant, we did learn to live simply and be content.

God began to rewire us.

As we lived on mission by discipling young adults and serving the poor, we grew more content and peaceful than ever before. We recognized our happiness was not attached to our possessions. Living simply and being content has very little to do with net worth; it's an attitude of the heart.

Living Within Our Means

JIMMY

Living within your means is the heart of contentment; it's also countercultural. Romans 13:8 says to "owe nothing to anyone except to love one another." Proverbs 22:7 states, "The borrower becomes the lender's slave."

We decided early in our marriage to live debt-free. Our kids grew up in an environment where we paid cash for virtually everything. If we used a credit card, we always paid it off at the end of the month. Living debt-free changed our lifestyle. Shopping was not a hobby, and going out to eat was a rare treat when the kids were young. We waited to purchase big items because we saved up over time rather than purchasing on credit.

It sounds difficult, but was actually a lot of fun. We enjoyed involving our kids as well. When we needed something but didn't have the cash, we told them and then explained how it was a great opportunity to see God provide, or a great opportunity to learn patience. We celebrated financial breakthroughs together, and we developed patience. Above all, our whole family learned contentment.

Feeling called to missions, we lived simply in order to be ready to move overseas if the Lord led us. As a result, we rented a home for sixteen years. Some questioned our decision by telling us we were throwing away money in rent every month. We saw it differently, feeling we were paying for our freedom to follow God's leadership.

Years later, our church moved to the inner city. We also moved and built our first home on a vacant lot in a poor, crime-ridden neighborhood near the church. While we sought God about living as missionaries overseas, we felt led to live missionally in our own city.

Our family's greatest financial challenge was to build this house using only cash. We started with a few thousand dollars and an incredible group of friends. We spent countless weekends clearing the lot, framing the house, and installing insulation—paying for everything as we went along.

As the days went on there were key times when we needed a specific amount of money to move forward. At the beginning of one particular month we knew that in two weeks we needed $18,000 to continue the house. After paying our bills there was nothing left. I went on a jog that morning and found 7 cents—a nickel and 2 pennies. We gathered the kids together for family devotions. I got a jar down from the kitchen cabinet, put the money in it, and said, "Kids, we have two weeks to see $18,000 come in. We now have 7 cents towards our goal. Let's pray and trust God for the rest. Let's do it together." We told everyone in the family that we were going to clean out the pantry and the fridge for our daily meals. We were going to be frugal on how we spent our money so that every extra penny that came in could go to seeing this house built. The kids jumped in fully. They ran through the house and looked in the chairs and couch cushions and came back with $1.52. We were well on our way! We just needed $17,998.41. As the week went on the kids each came to us individually and gave money they had been saving. We sold a couple of things, bringing us to a few hundred dollars.

And then it happened! A big encouragement came in. When the mail came on this particular day, we opened a letter from longtime friends of ours who were missionaries overseas. They had given their lives sacrificially for the last ten years, but had consistently struggled financially. Laura and I and the kids had supported them monthly for those ten years. In the letter they told us about a small inheritance they had received. As they prayed about it they felt that God was directing them to give a portion of it to us. They sent us a check for $11,000! To say the least, we were rejoicing together in God's encouragement and provision. Over the next two weeks we would see the whole $18,000 come in. It was fun, it was sacrificial, and it was a team effort. I thought it was so interesting that the largest gift for that need did not come from someone's abundance but through dear friends that we had invested in for years that were looking for an opportunity to give back. Experiences like this shaped our kids' lives.

Though difficult, living debt-free produced amazing fruit in our kids. They learned the value of money and patience. They learned to seek God's provision rather than feed materialistic desires. Ultimately, they experienced the freedom found in living a debt-free life.

GIVE GENEROUSLY

With the money we received, we taught our kids the joy and obedience of tithing as a first priority. Proverbs 3:9 says, "Honor the Lord from your wealth and from the first of all your produce." They began tithing with the first money they earned, from their allowances and other jobs. We also instructed them to set aside 10% for missions and 10% for savings. Two of our kids went even further and set aside 10% for the poor, leaving the remaining 60% or 70% for their own use.

This shaped their financial mindset, establishing God and others as the first priority, savings as the second, and personal consumption last. They found when they gave abundantly to others, God provided abundantly back to them. We encouraged each of our kids not just to give consistently but to give extravagantly. All of them took opportunities to pray for every situation and would give what they felt like God was leading them to do.

One day when Lauren was in high school, she came to us and said she felt that she was to give $500 to one of her friends so that she could go on an upcoming mission trip. Though we were thankful for her generous heart, we questioned the extravagance. You see, she only had $500 for her own trip, and $800 was due in the next week. Laura and I prayed about it ourselves and we thought, "Well, we have always said you can't outgive God and we have trained our kids to be generous.

Even if Lauren is not able to go and the other girl does, she will still have the joy of giving." Lauren gave the $500 anonymously to her friend, and within a week both of them had the $800 they needed. Teaching your kids to give abundantly is at times uncomfortable, but our kids have found it not only a joy but also a resource for their own future needs. When we tithe and give to others first, we experience the joy of partnering with God and we receive the blessing of His provision.

Remember, our culture teaches us the opposite. We're bombarded by advertisements designed to foster discontentment. We're challenged by well-meaning advisors to prioritize our own financial stability. These messages fly at us constantly. But the Bible teaches a different way; God challenges us to give first and trust Him as our Provider. This is an act of faith. Whom will we serve? Whom do we trust?

We do not regret living differently than the world. We do not regret teaching our kids to value God and others more than their own needs. Our decision to live this way was costly, but it was money well-spent.

INTEGRITY

A righteous man who walks in his integrity—
How blessed are his sons after him.
Proverbs 20:7

I once went out to eat with Daniel when he was six years old. When I received the bill, I was surprised to see the total was only $10. I reviewed it and discovered they only charged for my meal and not his. Rather than simply paying the mistaken amount, I saw the situation as a wonderful teaching moment.

I explained the mistake to Daniel and described our response, "We could walk out of here. We could even consider this mistake to be a blessing from God. But that is not right. The owners of this restaurant set the prices in order to take care of their family. It's honorable and right before God to communicate when we're undercharged."

Together, we walked back, explained the mistake, and paid the full amount. This is one of hundreds of similar experiences. Our consistent response communicated a clear lesson to our children: integrity is far more important than saving a dollar.

PREPARED FOR THE FUTURE

Lauren finished high school and set out to start college. She planned to serve as a missionary in India for a semester and return in the spring to start classes. Based on her hard work in high school, she received multiple scholarships. Our family gave sacrificially and reduced the tuition amount due to $3000.

Abby was already midway through her second year of college, all debt-free. However, Lauren's bill would soon be due, and we felt overwhelmed because we had no money left. In response, we called a family meeting. We drove to a nearby town so we could seek God together without distractions. .

In our discussion, Laura and I offered to work second jobs to pay the bills. We did not want them to feel the pressure of our finances. The kids unanimously responded by saying, "Mom and Dad, you didn't teach us to live like that. You taught us to live by faith, to work hard, to trust God."

They continued, "If anyone is getting a second job it is going to be us. It's time to establish our own stories of faith and not just live off of yours." We all began to cry. It was a holy moment for us as we saw this financial value take root in their hearts. We prayed together and left filled with faith.

Lauren's college tuition was due three days after our conversation. The next day I received a phone call from a friend who asked me to stop by his house. I assumed there was a problem and hoped everything was OK.

I walked into his house fully expecting to help him with a need, but was shocked to discover the real purpose of our visit. He sat me down and shared how God had prospered his business over the past year. He and his wife had prayed about how to bless others with their abundance and felt led to give toward our kids' education.

Overwhelmed with gratitude, I reluctantly took the envelope he offered, thanked him profusely, and walked out the door. When I arrived home and opened the envelope I pulled out a check for $3000, the exact amount due. He could not have known our need, but God knew. Not having all of our financial needs met enabled our family to seek God together and to recommit to living our basic financial values. God is faithful.

Because of our commitment to live simply, work diligently, and give generously, our life has been an adventure. We never lacked anything; in fact, God blessed us far beyond our need. But more importantly, our children developed a biblical value system that has given them the opportunity for a lifetime of contentment and success.

"When I graduated from high school, my parents had a party for me. They invited about a hundred of our family friends to celebrate. My Dad read a poem he had written called Better Man than I. In it he told me, and all who were listening, how I had become so much more than he could have imagined. That day I was more encouraged and called out than I have been any day before or since. A strong sense of identity was stamped on my heart once again by my parents who loved me. I knew they were proud of me."

CALEB

CHAPTER

18

DEFINING
MOMENTS

Your eyes have seen my unformed substance;
And in Your book were all written
The days that were ordained for me,
When as yet there was not one of them.
Psalm 139:16

JIMMY

Caleb's thirteenth birthday was a momentous occasion. He wasn't just turning a year older; he was going from a boy to a young man. It deserved special attention, so we spent months planning a father-son getaway where we could talk about his transition into adolescence while going on an out-of-town adventure.

It was going to be awesome: a plane to Florida for plenty of golf, some time on the beach, and even a couple of days at Disney World. What boy wouldn't be going crazy with excitement?

But then, right before the trip, Caleb got a cold, which quickly turned into a fever. We prayed hard, believing he would improve before we left, but things just went from bad to worse. By noon of the first day of the trip, his fever spiked even higher. He was congested and miserable.

"Why is God letting this happen?" he asked, with tears in his eyes.

I felt bad for him, to be sure, but I knew this was a teaching moment. "Caleb," I said, "we prayed and asked God to heal you, but it hasn't happened. So, you now have a choice. You can ask why and stay upset, or you can ask God to strengthen you through the challenge." I waited a moment for the words to sink in. "Son, this is a defining moment in your life. If you choose to trust God in the hard times instead of blaming God for your problems, you'll be able to endure anything that comes your way. Commit your situation to God, listen for direction, then move forward. Spending countless hours asking why or blaming God never works for anyone. God is faithful; sometimes we understand what He is doing, and sometimes we don't. But we can always trust that He is with us."

This may sound trite considering the bigger issues he will certainly face as an adult, but this moment provided a powerful life lesson neither he nor I will ever forget: *Don't blame God when things get hard; trust Him.*

Over the years, we've sought to consistently speak identity into our children. Different milestones in their lives have provided perfect opportunities to do so. These defining moments included birthday parties, learning to read, turning thirteen, graduations, and weddings.

Laura and I used special events, words of encouragement, and meaningful letters to mark these significant life transitions and reaffirm our kids' identity. We never regretted pausing long enough to truly celebrate each child.

BIRTHDAY PARTIES

LAURA

For the kids' birthdays I set aside time to bake a special cake that in some way symbolized the past year for them. From race cars to ballerinas, those cakes built memories among us all. I also brought their favorite takeout food and cupcakes to school and gathered their class to sing "Happy Birthday." We hosted a party at our house filled with games and creative themes. Before we cut the cake we told their birth story, recalled God's promises over their lives (sometimes to their embarrassment), and then shared ways we saw them grow in the character of God in the past year. As the kids grew older, we asked their friends to join in the time of encouragement. Though this sounds simple, these were moments to stop all of life and let them and their friends know how special they are to us. To this day the kids still talk about having the best birthdays of all their friends.

LEARNING TO READ

Learning to read was always a big deal in our family. Because we valued reading so much, we gave a special reward to symbolize the achievement.

When the kids were little, Jimmy frequently traveled

overseas to plant churches and serve our mission work. This created in our children a desire to go to the nations as well. In response, we started "Daddy/kid trips." Whenever our kids learned to read books on their own, they became a candidate to go on the next trip.

Over time our children witnessed ways God was moving all over the world. On these special trips, Daddy always added something unique to the itinerary. The kids slept in castles in Germany, traveled underground to the DMZ between North and South Korea, and golfed in Scotland.

Jimmy and I knew these trips were more than a simple reward for reading; they were defining moments in the lives of each of our kids.

MANHOOD AND WOMANHOOD TRIPS

JIMMY

Another rite of passage was a three-day trip to talk about sexuality and the pressures they would face in adolescence. We wanted to introduce the topic of their bodies changing, sexual desires, and the dangers of pornography before they learned it from their peers. Laura and I learned it from the culture, which is not the best teacher.

We sought to create an environment where our kids felt open to talk about sexuality with us instead of looking elsewhere for answers. We warned them about what they would hear out in the world and assured them they could talk to us about anything. All teenagers are curious, so we told them, "If you hear a conversation about a word you've never heard, please walk away from the conversation and come talk to us about it." By initiating the conversation before they were taught by their peers, and by creating an atmosphere of openness, we empowered them to take on the challenges of the world.

At an appropriate age, we took them on a trip to further the conversation without distractions. Laura took the girls individually, and I took the boys. We utilized curriculum such as Dr. James Dobson's *Preparing for Adolescence* and Dennis and Barbara Rainey's *Passport to Purity*. We also brought up the topic of dating, sharing about our own journeys and areas we struggled with during our teenage years.

We found this built trust with the kids and deepened our friendship with them. Our vulnerability about our childhood, as well as taking the time to listen and understand them, created a culture of openness. Conversations about sexuality and the challenges of being a teenager became a natural part of our interactions.

In addition to the trips, we wrote a letter to each child to mark the milestone of becoming a teenager. Here is part of the one I wrote for Caleb on his thirteenth birthday:

Dear Caleb,

From the day you were born, I have rejoiced in you being my son. There is no way to communicate in so few words my love and trust in you, or how proud I am of you. Still, I want to note a few things today.

1. *You are a man of great joy and contagious excitement. The Scripture says the joy of the Lord will be your strength. Your joyful zeal and excitement about life brings light into every room. Your smile, your love, your hugs, your enthusiasm has always brought joy not only to my heart but to so many around you.*

2. *You are a warrior at heart. In Numbers 13:10 when the 12 spies went out to the land, Caleb came back, he*

quieted the people and he said, "We should by all means go up and take possession of the land for we will surely overcome it." You are a warrior my son, one who believes in the impossible.

3. You are a man of worship and of intercession. David said this in Psalm 27:4, "One thing I have asked from the Lord, that I shall seek: that I may dwell in the house of the Lord all the days of my life." God has given you a heart for Himself. Your tenderness to God has been so evident, especially in the last few months as I have seen you come alive as a worshipper... From the time you were born your mom and I have prayed that you would be a worshipper and an intercessor, that through the songs that God gives you, you would sing over the people and would go before the people into the presence of the Lord. God has called you to be a worshipper and a man of prayer.

4. You are a faithful man. Thank you for being faithful to seek the Lord on a daily basis. For doing your schoolwork diligently, for taking the jobs that are before you and following through. For being disciplined and diligent in your athletics as well. God is growing this in you and every year I see you more faithful and more a man of diligence, one that others would want to follow.

I love being your dad and want to continue to learn to be your best friend. I am committed to you for life and want to be what you need and will do anything to help you succeed. I love you with all my heart and will stand with you as long as God gives me days on this earth. Not simply cheering from the stands but walking with you side by side, always standing with you and beside you.

Love,
Dad

SPECIAL GIFTS

Though Laura took the girls on their womanhood trips, I wanted to do something extra to mark the occasion as well. On Lauren's thirteenth birthday we told her to dress up because I wanted to take her out on the best date she had ever had. I took her to the nicest restaurant in town and we talked, joked, laughed, and had fun together. And then I pulled out this letter and read it to her:

My dearest Lauren,

From the day we knew Mom was pregnant, I have loved you and prayed for you. Your first cry with that little dimple melted my heart, and I have not stopped thanking God for giving me such a precious gift as you. It is hard to believe that it is your thirteenth birthday, as time seems to go so fast. But today I am thankful for the beautiful young woman you are. You are a woman of conviction, grace, love, compassion, purity, and security. God has forged in you a contentment and peace that draws His heart to you and the hearts of others to Him. You have been diligent in your studies, faithful in your friendships, and a perfect daughter and sister. When I talk about you to others I am so excited and proud. You are truly unique and wonderful, as you have chosen the Lord and His ways over all else. A dad could not be prouder. You are truly more than I could ever ask for, a complete joy to my heart.

I have prayed over you Psalm 27:1 and 2 Timothy1:7 that you would have great victory over the fears and challenges that come to you in this journey of love and life. I have prayed that you would encounter Jesus in a way that would capture your heart forever and that He would fill you with the knowledge of His will in every area of life. I will always be praying, encouraging, and supporting you as you follow the Lord in His will for you. I am committed to you for life and will always be here for you.

Today I am giving you a special ring. A ring to wear with joy and pride. A pledge to walk in purity and to save your heart and body only for God and the one He has for you in marriage. Wear it on your ring finger, and on your wedding day you'll replace it with a fresh commitment of love and faithfulness. This ring is our special bond of prayer and commitment to the Lord and one another.

I love you my precious daughter and am thankful to have a thirteenth birthday to remember for a lifetime.

Love,

Your Daddy forever

I slipped the ring on her finger and said, "This ring will only be replaced by a wedding ring. This is your commitment to purity and my commitment to pray and to stand with you and be there with you no matter what comes your way."

I earlier had the privilege of doing the same with Abby. These special bonding moments created a deeper commitment to one another and marked the transition from child to teenager.

Likewise, we bought James Avery cross necklaces for both Caleb and Daniel to signify our commitment together through this transition into the teen years.

SIXTEENTH BIRTHDAYS

Sixteenth birthdays represent an important milestone. It is the age when our kids received their coveted driver's license and newfound freedom. They become responsible for the power of a two-thousand-pound machine and with it gain a new range of freedom and choices. We taught our kids how to drive, but more importantly, how to navigate this new season of life.

We wrote another letter to celebrate this defining moment, sharing character traits we saw in them as well as warning them about the mistakes we made at their age. Here is mine to Daniel:

My dear Daniel,

First of all, let me say how thankful and grateful I am that you were born! Two years after we had Caleb, Mom became pregnant and had a miscarriage. Basically, that means the baby died and we lost it. We didn't know if we would be able to have another child, but God spoke to me so clearly that we would have another son and he would be blessed by God and he would be a blessing to others. And so two years later you were born to our great joy and delight.

When you were a little guy you were always so content and just wanted to be held and just simply to be by our side. Nothing could thrill my heart more than to be walking with you through life in whatever comes our way. Because of your gift in the area of golf, it has allowed us to spend literally hundreds of hours together travelling in the car, working through the challenges of the game, but more than anything else, my memories will always be walking down the fairway, side by side with you at places like Pinehurst or San Diego and praying for you every step of the way. God spoke to Mom and me early on that you would be gifted and your gift would make room for you to stand before great men, that God would cause you to stand before kings. And so it will be, my son.

On this, your sixteenth birthday, I want to communicate just a few things I wish I had known or done differently at sixteen.

1. I wish somebody would have told me to love Jesus and make Him a priority in my life by spending time with Him every day. That one thing has been the greatest choice I have ever made. If I would have done that at sixteen, less people would have been hurt and my life would have been cleaner and freer.

2. *I wish somebody would have told me that I had a gift on my life and that God was going to use me for His glory. When we live with that sense of identity and calling, there is a confidence and a clarity that helps us to make choices that build our lives toward changing the world and not just doing the next thing before us.*

3. *I wish somebody would have told me that relationships mattered more than my needs. When you build friendships and relationships with others, life is richer and more valuable. Every time you reach out to someone who is hurting or form a friendship with someone for mutual encouragement, you are adding richness and a depth to life that nothing else can, other than our personal relationship with Jesus.*

4. *I wish somebody would have told me that heaven was real and that the Kingdom of God is an adventure as we partner with Him in all the earth. Basically I wish somebody would have told me that the nations mattered to God. My son, you have been exposed to so many wonderful things and wonderful people. God has put an opportunity before you to learn and to grow and to invest and impact the nations of the world. If somebody would have told me that earlier, I would have spent my time and my energy on changing the world rather than living for myself.*

Let me end with a few other thoughts. Daniel, you are a man of faithfulness, both to God and to Mom and me. We are proud of you and so thankful for you.

You are a man of integrity. You do what you say you are

going to do and you honor your commitments.

You are a man of insight. I believe God has given you a gift of wisdom, just like He did Daniel in the Bible, and if you recognize that and open your mouth, you will be able to give insight and wisdom to people who are desperate for a word from the Lord.

I believe you are a man of influence. There is an anointing on your life to influence the people around you. God wants you to recognize that and to begin to exercise that at this time in your life.

And you are a man of contentment; a man of rest, one who is content in whatever he does.

And lastly, God has called you, my son, to be a man of excellence, to use the gifts of God whether it is the intellect you've been given, the athletic ability, or the opportunity to touch the nations of the earth. God wants you to use those gifts and, out of discipline and persistence, see people's lives changed and the nations rocked because you have given your heart to Him.

Happy sixteenth birthday my son! I love you more than you'll ever know and in some ways I am already missing the days and hours that we've had together, but I'm looking forward to a deeper relationship as we move forward as partners for the Kingdom.

In His strength and love,
Dad

HIGH SCHOOL AND COLLEGE GRADUATIONS

Graduations represent another stage in the journey of passing from youth into adulthood. We threw a large celebration for each child and invited teachers, family, and friends who influenced their lives. We created a video with pictures and highlights of their school years and asked a few people to speak words of affirmation. Following the encouragement we gathered to worship. We moved the graduate to the middle of the room and for the remainder of the evening our friends spoke blessings, encouragement, and ways they see them impacting their world. We recorded everything that was shared. These promises, encouragements, and words gave our kids great strength for the coming years.

WEDDINGS

We began this book with my memory of standing at the church doors with our daughter Abby on my arm, preparing to walk her down the aisle. In the days leading up to the ceremony, Laura and I spent time waiting on the Lord for encouragement to share with Kyle and Abby. We decided to give Kyle a compass engraved with Proverbs 3:5-6. Laura shared the affirmation that a compass always knows the direction, and as Kyle took the lead in their marriage, he would now lead their family. We gave this compass to remind him that God's will is always the right direction. Laura shared how she trusted him to care for our daughter and lead her further into God's will for her life than we ever could.

I also spoke encouragement to Kyle, my son-in-law. I was so proud of him. He and I had built a close relationship over the previous months. We vetted him thoroughly to make sure he was the right man to lead our daughter. We spent two decades as her covering and recognized the significance of this moment as we now entrusted this man with caring for her.

I still possessed Abby's first passport from when she was just five months old and we traveled overseas as a family. At her wedding rehearsal dinner, I shared the precious things I love about my dear daughter. After affirming her, I pulled out her old passport, handed it to Kyle and said, "Kyle, we raised her to touch the nations, we raised her to change the world, and now I am putting her into your hands. No pressure, buddy. But you are responsible for her from here on out. Now you guys will change the world together." And so they will.

There are thousands of opportunities for defining moments in the lives of your kids, but some possess extra special significance. Celebrate these moments to reinforce your kids' identity. Use these opportunities to mark the closure of one season and the beginning of another. Hopefully by sharing our kids' milestones we inspired you to celebrate yours. In the moment, life might feel crazy. Writing a meaningful letter or hosting a party may feel overwhelming when added to an already busy life, but we guarantee you will never regret giving time to truly celebrate the defining moments in your children's lives.

"As Abby and I began our dating journey, and to a large extent well before, I had a series of sit-downs with Jimmy/Dad. Even though I was asked some very blunt questions about my intentions with his daughter, as you would expect from any protective father, I always felt like I was being invited onto a journey and never excluded. As she and I started dating and eventually moved on to engagement and marriage, Jimmy/Dad continued to welcome me into the family as one of his own. During that year and a half, I gained a safe place to seek encouragement and wise council that I cherish to this day."

KYLE

19

DATING AND ATTRACTION

Watch over your heart with all diligence,
For from it flow the springs of life.
Proverbs 4:23

JIMMY

Our son-in-law, Kyle, asked me the day before the wedding if he could come out to address the audience before we began the actual service. After we talked about it I said, "Absolutely!"

Kyle stepped out in front of a thousand people waiting for the wedding to begin. He introduced himself and said hello and began to communicate what a special day it was. He shared about his own brokenness from his past and his need for Jesus. After coming to know the Lord in his late teens, he committed to walk in wholeness. He talked about his love for Abby and her purity. He shared with humility that he wished this was the same for him and yet, because of the grace of God, we were about to witness a holy moment. After they made their covenant with God, this would be her first kiss, and therefore, their first kiss. The covenant that they made today would be made out of purity and total dependence on God.

Wow! Laura and I were blown away, not only by Kyle's desire to share but also his commitment that had covered and protected Abby and brought restoration to him. You could feel the presence of God in that church and a sense of celebration and victory to see a young couple submitted to the ways of God and doing a relationship right. Kyle had committed to yielding to God in this relationship and walking out purity by practicing self-control, both by honoring God with his commitment and covering Abby with hers. It was beautiful.

You see, Laura and I grew up in normal America where love by physical expression became an option early on, and we took that option. Our ideas of relationships were just like you hear in songs on the radio or see in the movies, and we went with it. Of course our parents cautioned us to be moral and keep it clean, but there was not a why behind the charge. After finding Jesus, both of us adjusted a little bit but not that much. When we got to college and began to personally evaluate how we were doing relationships with the opposite sex, we realized that we had so easily given our hearts away and not protected ourselves or others in purity. We also found we had wasted so much time and ruined a lot of friendships because of our careless dating and actions. What we once thought was normal and cute and maybe going somewhere long term ended up gathering a lot of baggage and emotional wounds. Both were issues that we had to work through later to make our relationships work.

Our own journey out of brokenness from these past relationships has allowed us to help hundreds of college students as we began to hear their stories and to pastor them. We realized that most people were letting the world and not the Word of God dictate and teach them how to develop a relationship. The Word of God, in Song of Solomon 2:7, talks about not awakening love before its time. Proverbs 4:23 tells us above all else to guard our heart, for everything we do flows from it. These words, plus coaching with a lot of practical input, have spared many young people from broken hearts, sexual baggage, and wasted time.

We wanted so much freedom for our kids. We believed there was a great call on our kids' lives, and hopefully marriage was a part of that. And we wanted to navigate the journey as best we could in the healthiest way possible. We had experienced ourselves, and seen from so many others, the wasted emotions and time that go into "young love." We knew that wanting to be liked and liking someone would be two very normal emotions that our kids would be experiencing early on, and the world would be egging it on. We knew we needed a plan to help them guard their hearts and not awaken love before its time. So this was our journey.

BIRTH TO 5 YEARS OLD

We were committed to not putting anything before our kids that showed sensuality or even relationships in an inappropriate way. We highly monitored media so that they were not inundated with both images and ideas that would not be God's best for their little eyes. Maybe this is extreme, but one practical thing was that when the kids were little we would all turn our eyes when we saw someone kiss on the screen. This was our way of letting them know that God had made that for marriage, not just for casual love.

We were college pastors, so our kids were going to a lot of weddings and seeing the bride in her pretty dress and the excitement of the groom as he waited for his bride. They were experiencing the beauty of a wedding and the atmosphere of worship and a covenant made before God. This is what we wanted them to know as God's best, and we joyfully celebrated those moments with them.

At this age, we also began telling them that they could tell us about anything at any time, any feelings, anything that happened that they didn't feel good about, whether it was a friend or a babysitter (though we highly screened them all). We wanted to start a journey of being open with our feelings and questions they would have about relationships and sexuality.

We had to teach them what appropriate touching was and wasn't. We would tell them that nobody touches your private parts but Mommy or Daddy to help you if something is wrong, or a doctor as long as we are present. Other than that, no one touches you there and you don't touch anyone else there. This would lay a simple groundwork of healthy boundaries while they continued to grow and develop. It is normal for many children at this age to begin to explore themselves by touch- ing their private parts. At this age we wanted to keep it really simple but address it. We used simple language like, "We don't touch down there. That is a place where we go to the bath- room, and it's not healthy to play with it." We did not over- react and make a big deal about it, just tried to keep it simple and clear.

By the time they were kindergarten age we had to dialogue through the conversations of a boy or a girl coming up and saying "I love you" or "I like you." We communicated with them that it is normal to be attracted to a boy or a girl and at the right time God would have the right person for them, but at this point our stance would be to tell others, "We are just going to be friends." At this age, they are learning to build friendships with both boys and girls so that is what we would focus on.

ELEMENTARY SCHOOL

As they began to be involved in school and relationships with others, we encountered many other kids and families who had different values and different guidelines, so the communication had to be stepped up. We often shared with our kids that we were Seiberts and we were going to do things differently. We told them our whole goal was to protect them from things that we struggled with and to keep their hearts free from being distracted before it was time. Sometimes our kids were put into awkward situations with conversations about who liked whom. At this age, we encouraged them to kindly walk away. It wasn't worth where the talk was going or the possibility of it turning into gossip.

Once again, we made home a safe place and a refuge where we could talk about anything. Many times we were proactive about asking questions and giving them opportunity to share about what was going on in their hearts and with their peers.

LAURA

This was also the time when we started the talks about sex. Around fourth grade we explained to them about how babies are made. Just the basics. I remember going away with both of our girls at separate times and bringing up the subject. I had an age-appropriate book written by Dr. James Dobson. When I mentioned the word sex, even though I talked with them separately, neither of my girls had ever heard the word before. It sure was hard to keep the conversation going, but I knew that it was better to hear it from me than someone else, so I pressed through the uncomfortable conversation. The same was true for Jimmy and the boys. It was such a joy for us that the kids had made it this far in innocence and with a clean slate. That meant that guarding their media, being cautious of what they were exposed to, and being open to conversations had worked. We were able to protect their innocence and not create thoughts in their minds that weren't needed. We were able to start with a clean slate and began laying a solid, pure foundation.

Another situation that surfaced in elementary years was dealing with feelings of same-sex attraction. It can be normal, as kids develop sexually, to be interested or curious about the same gender as well as the opposite sex. It was important for us to not overreact to it as if something was wrong, but we would address it and say, "Hey, it's very normal to have feelings, but that does not determine who you are. God is clear in His Word that He made uniquely male or female, and that men are uniquely made for women and women for men." For our kids, this simple point of clarity set them free to enjoy who God made them to be. We know for different kids this may need to be a more in-depth conversation, but by going to God and His Word together in a loving environment, we will always find the answers to our unique parenting challenges.

JUNIOR HIGH

JIMMY

I remember overhearing Caleb talk to his seventh grade friends about who they liked or who they wanted to date. They asked him, "Caleb, who do you like?" He said, "I don't like anybody. I'm friends with everyone." His friends said, "Are you gay?" and he said, "Absolutely not. That is not the way God has made me. But I think it is stupid to think about dating somebody when you're not ready to be married." I thought, "Way to go, buddy!" He got it.

Even when in junior high they began to be around more people who were dating, we just kept our basic standards. We also began to open up a little bit about our own journey in dating and what we wish we had done differently. So many times we said, "Hey, I doubt you are going to marry any of these peers, so just enjoy making friends and having a good time." We still continued to help them navigate media, literature, books, and obviously coached them on the dangers of pornography. We put controls on their media resources and limited their amount of Internet.

We never shied away from who they were attracted to or how they felt about a person. We even took the opportunity to ask if there was someone they were singling out that they thought they liked and we had a conversation about it. We knew this was healthy and normal, but we continued to steer them toward building strong, healthy friendships. The less we made of it, the smaller the issue became.

HIGH SCHOOL

LAURA

When the kids were in high school, things obviously began to heat up in every direction. Here we began to really let them into our lives, and we fully talked about the things that we went through on our own journeys of relationships and dating. We openly shared how we had given our emotions away and even physically done things we later regretted. We both shared how we wasted so much time wanting to be liked and giving our hearts away to others.

We encouraged them to go to dances or proms in groups and with friends who shared their values. We personally gave them resources to help them research what they believed and wanted to own for themselves. One of the books they read was I Kissed Dating Goodbye by Joshua Harris (Multnomah, 1997), and another was The 10 Commandments of Dating by Ben Young and Samuel Adams (Thomas Nelson, 1999). We introduced them to both sides of the issue and let them decide for themselves, with our help, what was best.

We encouraged them to keep their hearts first for Jesus and then invest in healthy friendships. Because we started from the earliest age talking to them about the "why" behind guarding your heart, all of our kids chose not to date in high school. It kept the drama low and for that we are thankful.

OVER EIGHTEEN

As of this writing, we have one daughter who is married and our other two oldest have each been out on several dates. They have walked in purity and are a catch for anyone. (No, I am not being biased.) The only one yet to join in is our sixteen-year-old, and he is on his high school journey.

As our kids turned into adults we still continued to help them navigate this process. We have empowered our adult children to make quality decisions of their own such as where they want to live, what career path they want to choose, personal financial decisions, etc. We have asked that in the area of relationships they would still invite our counsel and input because who they marry will affect the rest of their lives (and ours too!).

This is our journey. Of course, we know that somewhere in your kids' journeys, dating will begin to happen. Whatever path your family chooses to follow, stay engaged, keep the conversations going, and pray a lot!

"When you are surrounded by the mission of world evangelization, life feels urgent and time feels precious. We were trained to make life count. And that meant intentional planning, using our time how God wanted us to, and not wasting a season. Though planning was annoying and tough as a kid—we had lots of family planning times with us bored and uninterested—now I could not be more grateful for having those habits instilled into me! I naturally make goals in each area of life and make a plan to get there. My parents showed me that though other young people may not seem to have a plan, in the words of my Dad, "No one changes the world by being like everyone else."

LAUREN

CHAPTER 20

FOCUSED AND INTENTIONAL

"So teach us to number our days,
That we may present to You a heart of wisdom."
Psalm 90:12

JIMMY

"Oh no, Dad, do we have to?" was a common response whenever I joyfully announced it was time for "Roles and Goals." Three times a year, at the beginning of each school semester and the summer, each member of our family clarified his or her roles in life and set specific goals for the next season. Not everyone enjoyed this exercise, especially the highly spontaneous ones in our family like Laura, but it became an expectation, and overall everyone was thankful.

LAURA

As Jimmy said above, I am a very spontaneous person and to be able to plan ahead or see into the future is really difficult. So when it came to creating roles and goals, it was super hard to do and came with much internal resistance. However, I knew through experience that it's hard to accomplish much or stay on track when you don't have a plan, so I, too, learned this was good for us all.

JIMMY

Despite their protests, I firmly believed we needed to live intentionally in order to accomplish our calling. As we often hear and experience, "The urgent takes over the important in life." This would happen to us for sure, as our life was very full. This exercise helped to slow us down and align us to what matters most.

In Acts 13:36, Luke declared that King David "had served the purpose of God in his own generation, fell asleep, and was laid among his fathers." David made mistakes, but ultimately he fulfilled his calling. This is my desire; I want the same to be said of me and of my family.

Paul further developed this theme in Ephesians 5:15-17: "Therefore be careful how you walk, not as unwise men but as wise, making the most of your time, because the days are evil. So then do not be foolish, but understand what the will of the Lord is." His readers grew to become a great church that eventually exerted influence throughout the whole world.

People do not change the world through good intentions alone. Lasting impact occurs when specific goals align with vision. Laura and I believe we would drift from our calling unless we intentionally set aside time to reset our focus on what matters most.

Our process of focusing on our calling began with the question, "What Scripture communicates what God is speaking to you for this season of your life?" When the kids were little, I would sit by them and help them discover the answer and write it at the top of their "Roles and Goals" paper. As they grew older we would pass out the paper and ask them to take time during their morning devotions to ask God what Scripture He was highlighting at this season in their life. They would use it as a guideline for each specific area of their life.

SPECIFIC CATEGORIES OF FOCUS
Spiritual Focus

We discussed basic spiritual disciplines such as worship, prayer, Bible reading, discipleship, and evangelism. The kids responded by writing down one or two things they felt God was highlighting for the semester. Many times this helped facilitate deep and meaningful conversations about their spiritual lives. Just pausing long enough to evaluate kept their spiritual lives vibrant and growing. Here are a few questions we regularly asked:

What is your time with Jesus going to look like over these next four months?

What is your Bible reading plan?

How are you going to share your faith?

Who are you discipling?

How can we help you spiritually?

What is a heart attitude you are dealing with?

Mental Focus

We initially included a mental growth category because we wanted our children to develop into avid readers. We asked them what books they wanted to read in the upcoming season or, at times, set a numeric goal for books to read. As part of accomplishing this goal, we signed up for the reading clubs at school or the library.

As mentioned earlier, once each child learned to fully read on their own and actually enjoyed chapter books, we rewarded them by giving them the opportunity to travel with me on one of my overseas ministry trips. We knew there would be a lot of meetings that they would have to be happy sitting quietly in between adventures and other fun things we could do, so enjoying reading was a value. This usually happened around eight years old. This was a highly coveted and long-awaited trip for each child, so reading became a goal to accomplish.

This category of focus also covered practical things that take time and effort to learn, such as riding a bike, making a craft, sewing a dress, or playing the guitar. The act of writing down the goal created accountability for us to work together.

Caleb once wrote that he wanted to learn to play the guitar. We helped him achieve his goal by signing him up for lessons. His tutor, our worship leader, asked him to practice fifteen minutes a day. Caleb hated practicing and resisted the discipline it required. He cried and complained. In the low moments, we consistently reminded him of his goal. "This is something you felt God wanted you to do, and we want to support you. You cannot live by your emotions. Instead you must learn to be diligent and faithful with what you feel God has spoken to you." It took about a year for him to really enjoy learning to play. Today Caleb is a worship leader. It is his greatest joy. He is reaping the benefits of pushing through and accomplishing what he wrote down as a God-inspired skill he wanted to develop. Little did he know it would become his passion. Learning something new is hard and takes a lot of work. This is a perfect example of listening to God and setting goals to follow through with so our emotions don't rule.

Family Focus

One of our personal goals as parents is to stay close as a family. We used the Roles and Goals process as a sweet time of reaffirming our desire to grow close as a family. We asked questions like:

How will we spend time together and be involved in one another's lives?

What challenges or issues are we having with a sibling or a parent?

How are we going to get closer in this next season?

These honest and loving conversations gave everyone an opportunity to share their feelings and helped us respond by creating a plan to grow. We wrote down action items, including things like, "I need to be nicer to my brother or sister and play more with them," "I need to pray for my siblings," "I need to help Mom more around the house," and "I need to write or call Grandma once a week."

Growth as a family required intentionality in our relationship. The combination of periodic evaluation and specific action steps helped us not to plateau in our relationships with one another, which is easy to do.

Relationship Focus

We all need friends, but we're limited by time and space. We can't be friends with everyone, so we need to focus on developing relationships with a few. Laura and I wanted to help our kids make quality decisions in their friendships and in their care for others who might not have as many friends. We asked questions like:

Who do you enjoy playing with and want to spend more time with?

Who needs you to be their friend during this season?

Is there anyone in your life who does not know Jesus who you can reach out to?

We wrote down their responses and then worked together to develop an action plan in order to cultivate meaningful relationships.

Financial Focus

In the previous chapter we discussed how we trained our kids in the basic discipline of managing their finances. During our Roles and Goals time we applied these principles and created an action plan for the upcoming season, asking things like:

What events are coming up, and how much will they cost?

What portion will you pay, and what are Mom and Dad going to take care of?

How will you work to earn the money that is needed during this season?

These answers changed with time, but even at a young age we worked together to help our kids with their finances. Our kids set specific financial goals for things they both needed and wanted and worked hard accordingly. We were also clear of how we would partner together and what our portion would be toward their desired activity or need.

Physical Focus

LAURA

Both Jimmy and I knew that physical activity and staying in shape is a habit that is learned by most people, not naturally given. We wanted our kids to value exercise and staying in shape so they will have the strength to do what God has called them to do. Of course, with each one it was at different levels and different intensities, but we knew we wanted it to be a value. So, we encouraged our kids to set exercise goals. If they played a sport, we wanted them to be disciplined in practice. They set goals such as a specific number of baskets to shoot every day or laps to swim or miles to run. After they set the goal, we mapped it out to help them achieve it.

Time Focus

After setting goals, we took our great ideas and placed them into a schedule to see if they were realistic. Sometimes we set too many goals and had to eliminate a few. Other times, we determined we could do even more than we'd listed. If you set too many goals you won't achieve them and might end up discouraged, which defeats the whole purpose. If we set too few, we found that we wasted time and ended up doing too many things that had no value.

While we sought to support our kids' passions, we also felt we needed to hold them accountable to follow through. I've often seen parents back off challenging their kids because of the inconvenience of accountability or because their child got mad. The process of setting aside time every four months to plan helped us work together for our kids' personal growth.

Unless someone has been given an incredibly self-motivated child and one that is incredibly organized, in reality it is really difficult for a child to get where they want to be unless they have help. Our role as parents is to help coach them to discover their gifts and callings and then take the steps to get them there. Intentionality is inconvenient, and accountability is not always enjoyable; but as parents, we will not regret paying the price to see our children become responsible adults.

CHAPTER 21

WHERE DO WE GO FROM HERE?

But by the grace of God I am what I am, and His grace toward
me did not prove vain; but I labored even more than all of
them, yet not I, but the grace of God with me.
1 Corinthians 15:10

JIMMY

I was sitting in a room with twenty-five men who all had given
a million dollars in personal wealth to causes here in America
and around the world. It was truly a privilege to sit there with
these incredibly generous and gifted leaders and influencers.
I was there because a friend had asked me to come and share

our story of walking with God, specifically about how we started the church and raised a family around the three simple principles of living simply, working diligently, and giving generously.

As the evening went on, after sharing our story, it was question and answer time. Quickly the questions shifted from "How can we be good stewards of our finances?" to "How do you raise great kids?" I was surprised at how engaged they were as I talked about each of our children and how we tried to raise them, not just in dealing with finances, gifts, and talents, but how they could be contributors to society.

For some there was noticeable pain in the questions they asked as they talked about their families and the regrets they had. Others were inquisitive because they were on the front end of the journey. But leaving that evening I was struck by one thing: every parent cares more about their kids making it than they care about making it themselves. When the day is done, we all want a strong family. We all want a healthy family. We all want a loving family. This book was not written with the illusion that ours, or any other family, will be perfect; rather if we would put raising our kids and developing our family as a top priority around God and His Word, there would always be grace to endure whatever comes our way. More than fame or fortune, people care about family.

THE GRACE OF GOD

So where do we go from here? Obviously you are reading this book because you have a desire to love your family and move them forward. I want to make sure, if it hasn't been fully communicated yet, that this is done only by the grace of God.

I often teach about grace, and when I do I communicate two definitions. Grace is the love, pleasure, and favor of God toward undeserving people. It is also the power of God to do the will of God. Grace is like a multifaceted diamond that empowers us and strengthens us and gives us hope, forgiveness, and a new start even when we don't deserve it.

Grace-Centered Parenting

When grace is at the center of our parenting, we can come to the end of our lives and see that God truly has been faithful. When Laura and I first started out, as we mentioned, we did not know what we were doing. So we came to God by His grace and humbled ourselves. We, over and over again, prayed and asked Him to help us, guide us, lead us, and direct us. We believed that God would lead us by His voice and by His wisdom if we would simply listen and put our hearts out before Him on a daily basis. Even to this day I am so amazed that when we come before God on a daily basis we'll have a sense of what one of our adult children need or we'll have a sense of how to counsel or not counsel them as they continue to develop and grow.

Laura and I also realized that we needed a new framework, a new paradigm to look at, to know how parenting should be done. The Word of God is that guide for us. From the stories of the Old Testament with things done right and things done wrong, to the Proverbs and wisdom of how to live life, to the life of Jesus and the New Testament church, we have found that the Word of God speaks directly to any and every situation that comes our way. By allowing the Word to be the initial foundation of our parenting journey, we had a place to go back to, a place to sift through all ideas and books we read and thoughts that people had. We knew that if we could go back to the Word of God there would always be grace—the power to be able to raise our kids in a way that would be healthy, life-giving, and for their benefit.

Grace Is Forgiveness

I was talking the other day to a couple whose kids are grown, and now they are beginning to experience the joys of becoming grandparents. They were asking, "What were the key issues in raising your family? What were the difference-makers for you and Laura in raising kids?" and I found the first thing coming out of my mouth was, "We were willing to repent."

If there was anything we wanted to be great at, it was humbling ourselves to our kids, asking forgiveness, and extending forgiveness to them. One of the things we found out early on was that our kids never had the expectation that we would be perfect, they just wanted us to be loving and warm and wanted us to be close. By choosing to ask forgiveness and receive forgiveness from one another from their youngest age to the present, we have found that God uses that environment of humility toward one another to allow us to navigate and work through any issue. When we as parents have done anything wrong, we can always go back to our kids, ask for forgiveness, and believe God for a fresh start.

Grace Is Community

The power of grace is not only found through seeking God individually and as a couple, but grace is also found in community. We saw the grace of God in other families. We saw it in other friends who cared enough to speak into our lives when they felt we were doing things wrong as well as affirm us when we were doing things right. It was this grace given through community that kept us strong and focused in the marathon journey of parenting.

None of us were made to live alone, and no family was meant to raise their kids in isolation. It is gathering with a group of believers, called the church, that gives us eyes, ears, hands, and help in the journey. Laura and I often comment that it seems many times people are open to correction in every area except with their kids. My encouragement is to draw near to one another. Wrestle through issues together; learn together so that the grace of God can abound in you while your children are connecting to a group of like-minded people. This is where you will find strength for the journey.

Grace Is Redemption

One of the big questions that we often are asked is, "We have already messed up. We have already raised our kids. What do we do?" This is the greatest news in the world. It is the good news of the life of Jesus: there is always forgiveness, there is always hope, and there is always a new day. There are certain consequences that linger in our lives and in our kids' lives because of mistakes made along the way. But God can take the most broken places in us and make them our greatest places of ministry and our greatest places of grace.

Dan and Mercedes Peters were great mentors for us early in our marriage. Mercedes had seven children, and Dan had eight. Neither of them knew the Lord and ended up in a relationship with one another outside of their existing marriages. Their original marriages ended in divorce, and they eventually married. They had another child together to make a total of sixteen children and seriously realized they needed help; they needed Jesus. Not only did they need Jesus, but they needed every part of the Word of God working in their lives. As they began to see God working, they also saw that there were many others that needed help in their marriages and families.

Mercedes felt a call to lead, guide, and direct other women. She started a Bible study that met weekly, and she would give them homework to complete during the week. She talked about what it means to be a wife and a mother. Dan began to teach classes on what it means to be a husband by leading your family in holiness, loving your wife, and working hard. Literally hundreds of men and women were affected by their teaching, by their training, and by their diligence to seek God and His Word. Now in their later years, they have seen the incredible, redeeming hand of God in using their broken lives to be able to bless and strengthen so many. Of those sixteen kids, not everything has turned out perfect. There are still issues and challenges Dan and Mercedes have had to work through from their past struggles. But God took their greatest place of weakness and used it not only for victory in their lives, but to help others find victory in their own lives. If they had decided that their influence was over because they had already messed up and they had no right to help other people, I believe many families would not be in the healthy place that they are today.

Moms and dads, in our journey in this world, there will always be challenges and there will always be struggles. But we have a perfect God who loves us and forgives us and empowers us to live lives that tell the story of His faithfulness. The redemption and forgiveness of God is so powerful and so real that it can take your greatest place of brokenness and make it your greatest place of victory. Hand in hand with God, you are free to start your own journey of parenting without regret.

NOTES

NOTES

CONNECT WITH US AT

WEBSITE: ANTIOCHCC.COM

TWITTER: @JIMMY_SEIBERT

FOREWORD BY **MAX LUCADO**

PASSION & PURPOSE

BELIEVING THE CHURCH CAN STILL CHANGE THE WORLD

JIMMY SEIBERT